CONNECTING

How to Stop Losing and Start Winning in Love

by
Kenneth Schulman

Symphony Press, Inc.
Tenafly, New Jersey

TABLE OF CONTENTS

Page

People Want You To Love Them

People want you to love them, even if they don't show it. After all, there is nothing more flattering or more gratifying than being loved. If you can convince the object of your affections to feel comfortable accepting your love, they may very well learn to love you in return.

Even the haughtiest, most independent men and women want you to break through the barriers they've set up and lavish love and attention upon them. Sometimes men and women who have defined models of who their lovers should be are astonished to discover the most unlikely people have entered their lives and their hearts.

When Jay joined the Forward Toy Company, he had everything going for him. He is tall, dark, handsome, thirty-two, single, drove a silver Porsche, and had just been imported from New York to set up a direct mail division which everyone hoped would stimulate sales of Forward's famous stuffed animals.

The ladies of the company practically lined up for inspection, each one vying for the new trophy. Jay enjoyed flirtations, wistful eye contact, smiles, and a few outright propositions. He told me he felt like a six foot, stuffed animal they wanted to take home.

Nancy, one of the assistant buyers, was as attracted to him as the other women, she just expressed it

1

differently. Nancy is neither pretty or homely. At best, she had a healthy, physical presence, and lovely strawberry blonde hair. She is also a genuinely kind, considerate person.

Perhaps Nancy felt more deeply about Jay than the other women, or maybe she felt he needed something more satisfying than a good lay. I think she instinctively understood the power of love and used it to her advantage without the least connivance.

She thought about Jay; she considered the fact that he was a stranger in Detroit. She began her contact with him by suggesting lunch places and shops in the area. She also got him coffee when she went for her own. Nancy brought him the novel *Shogun* and told him how much she loved reading it, even though it took her the entire summer.

And Nancy encouraged him to talk to her when he had an obviously rough day. She didn't come on strong in a sexual way and she never invited him over for dinner. But she did show a loving concern that cut straight through to his heart. She knew that he wanted to be loved and wasn't afraid to show that she loved him. Soon he stopped thinking about Lisa's legs and Rachel's breasts and started concentrating on Nancy's love. Jay wasn't exactly afraid of love, he just wasn't used to it. But it didn't take him long to learn.

Many people don't think they can love. Some because they never did before, others because they aren't sure whether the feelings they experienced can actually be called "love."

Love is an ambiguous term because so many of us use it in different ways and with varying degrees of intensity.

This confusion has existed for quite a while, it seems. The greatest minds have been puzzled because it doesn't happen in the head, it can't be diagnosed with logic. It is emotional, something we each feel in our own way.

People speak of infatuations, sexual liaisons, lust, companionship, friendship — but not love. That magical four letter word without which none of us feels complete.

If you encounter one of these unfortunates and you care for him or her, your heart should go out to them. Whether or not they are willing to admit it, they are frustrated and they are suffering. The failure to love, as Eric Fromm reminds us, leads to destruction — self-destruction or the destruction of others.*

But if you extend your hand or better still your heart, you can unlock the love that lies within us all. Love has the power to create love. Love instills love. Love inspires love. If you don't already know it, love is a magic power. By using it properly, that is by setting a loving example, we can bring it out in others.

Most people feel alienated in today's society. Urban living and working conditions are cell-like and the remoteness of nature only aggravates our feelings of isolation. That's why we have to make even more of an effort to connect, to communicate and to extend ourselves.

*Fromm, Eric, *The Art of Loving*

Most of us are well-fed, well-dressed, even sexually satisfied. But without love we cannot be happy.

When Lynn met John, he was a misanthrope, a hermit, and a recluse. His job as a proof-reader allowed him to maintain this anti-social attitude. An automobile accident left him with a limp, a dented forehead and a ton of hostility. When he got an intense toothache his disposition reached rock bottom but that's how he met Lynn, a dental assistant.

Lynn liked John without feeling sorry for him. He interpreted her friendliness as part of the job. John felt that no one could love a man with a dented head and he set up a wall of hostility six inches thick to keep out the pity, ridicule, and rejection. It was like the Guardol shield we used to hear so much about in tooth paste commercials.

Lynn is tall, slender and pleasant looking in a wry, twinkly sort of way. John is also tall and slim, has shining reddish hair and a Don Rickles approach to life that never failed to make Lynn laugh.

Watching Lynn's face light up sparked something deep inside John's morose soul. After several visits to the dentist and several encouraging remarks from Lynn, John realized she actually liked him and wasn't just doing her job. He was a tough nut to crack but Lynn's patience and kindness broke through his cynical shell. John had guarded his loving feelings for so long, it took time for them to surface.

Lynn understood that John sometimes acted nasty

4

just to test her, but she hung in there like a stubborn molar. Her compassion and sincere admiration for his mind eventually won him over.

When he realized she was for real, he slowly began to relax the tight security he had imposed over his tenderness. John felt love for the firt time and he was overwhelmed.

I had a squirrel monkey who was usually scared stiff. He put up a good front, though, even tried to bite the hand that fed him — mine. Persistence, calmness and unselfishness eventually got through to the little fellow. I didn't stop to think, I'm giving so much and he's still hostile and unresponsive. I never considered my own ego because I understood all along that the monkey was scared and needed help.

People are much trickier than monkeys because they don't always look scared. Sometimes they look scary. It's hard to imagine that some big lug can be terrified of a petite little women, but he can. For all his bulk, his feelings may be just as fragile.

I was ogling a lovely woman the other day in the supermarket. Our carts passed several times and I was smitten. On the fourth pass, she smiled at me. I still can't get over the fact that I froze up and looked hostile instead of happy. It was actually my fear that appeared to be hostility. Naturally, she thought I was mean and quickly pushed her cart away.

We're all afraid to extend ourselves, expose our bare wires and have them snipped. Rejection is very painful.

That's why everyone needs reassurance and support instead of a display of egos.

If you really want to crack that seemingly unfeeling, unloving wall, play sweet soulful music and keep it coming soft and mellow. Eventually it goes over, under or through the thickest of walls. They all have chinks you know. Remember how well Joshua did at Jericho?

Obviously you must feel that the object of your affection is worth such an effort. It's not always easy to be loving, especially when the feeling isn't reciprocated. At least you have the satisfaction of knowing you are a generous human being. Think of how satisfying it will be when you gradually wear down that resistance and the love is finally returned.

I have been amazed to see my own relationships grow and blossom into love when they began with nothing more than mild interest and sexual desire.

To know that someone genuinely loves you is a wonderful feeling. So wonderful, you usually want to love in return. Perhaps not for all time but taken one day at a time, it may take you a lot farther than you expect.

Project Your Sex Appeal

How can someone who is basically shy and ordinary looking get attention? Answer: Sex appeal.

Sex appeal is the single most compelling force that brings people together. It is a magic magnet that activates from time to time. And when it happens, it can cause an ache in the pit of the stomach, a flutter in the heart, and a heightened body temperature causing the well known flush of excitement. These symptoms are very individual but they are there in each of us — to be received as well as sent out.

In order to project your sex appeal, you must know what makes you feel sexy. If you know, you are ahead of the game. If you don't, think of people you consider sexy and try to decide why.

I think it boils down to a genuine love of love-making. If you enjoy sex and look like you are ready, willing and able to prove it, people are going to notice. To me, there is nothing more stimulating than availability.

Men are known to be the classic aggressors but the seemingly reticent female may in reality be more aggressive by making the move that signals her availability.

Whether male or female, availability is fundamental. To achieve this you must do more than *act* available, you must really be available. Come to terms with this and you'll probably start feeling sexier immediately. What you must communicate is that you are ready.

7

In addition to availability, the second most potent source of sex appeal is passion. When it is surging below the surface, it sets off a chain reaction that can end in a powerful love affair.

Passion makes the prize appear richer and more rewarding.

Elaine M. is not a great looking lady but she has a love of life that is contagious. She's in her late twenties, has medium brown hair, an athletically stocky body and an everpresent smile. Her attitude is what I think of as Roman but she is just a healthy mid-western girl with an openly hedonistic passion for life.

Whether it is a good book, a good softball game, party, song, or glass of wine, she seems to squeeze the last ounce of enjoyment for it and cheerfully toss it over her shoulder. You just know she'd be a great lover. And you want to find out.

Granted, not all of us are lucky enough to have her unabashed joy of living. We have inhibitions and feelings of guilt. We are afraid to make fools of ourselves.

We should work on changing all that. It's not impossible. Just do what makes you happy. Then do more of it. Feel the pleasure and revel in it. Don't hide it.

And if it doesn't come naturally, manufacture it. Jon H. is a middle man in the textile industry. Thirties, tall, thin, an indoor man, happier listening to records than birds.

Jon once told me he used to sit opposite dates feeling terribly cowed because the woman was good looking and self assured. "They made me feel like a schlepper by comparison. Sometimes, I'd feel so intimated, I felt totally sexless. I could feel my pecker getting smaller and smaller. Actually retreating. Then one time at a restaurant, I stopped listening to what we were talking about and just looked at her. Her hair, her eyes, her beautiful ears, lips and breasts. I reached down into my inner being and tried to find my sexuality. I would try to start feeling horny, lusty and turned on.

When I was able to do this, when I did manage to conquer my feeling of utter helplessness and sexlessness, then I would try to communicate this with my eyes.

I would look her directly in the eyes and with all my strength, I would try to send messages of animal lust from my eyes to hers. To my amazement, it worked like magic. I psyched myself up much like a professional athlete before a big game. It may not work for everyone but it sure helped me."

What makes you feel sexy? Almost anything is possible: shiny hair, a clear complexion, a tough game of squash, a shower, soft-clingy clothes, a hair cut, or a business success. The sexier you feel the more readily others will pick it up.

Many people are afraid to by sexy. They think people will scorn them for being obvious, or because they are afraid of sexual failure. One solution to this problem is to seek professional help. Another suggestion is to decide that this is just one more fear that must be faced down. And the best way to defeat it is to take chances.

Some people are better lovers than others. So what? You don't have to be the best, you just have to be good. Fortunately, we all have the capacity to satisfy one another. Men and women have been at it for thousands of years. They knew how to do it centuries ago and very little has changed.

Look at almost any man or woman. No matter how attractive or remote they appear, just remember — if you were both stranded on a desert island, it would just be a matter of time before you would have them moaning in ecstasy. If you wanted to. Know this is true and remind yourself the next time your courage slackens or those old insecurities rear their ugly heads. You don't have to be beautiful or handsome to satisfy someone. Just willing to use the instincts and techniques stored deep inside you.

Certain timid souls, have nothing but admiration for blatantly sexy people.

"Oh it's all right for them to be that way, because the woman in the black satin gown or the guy in the suede slacks *really is sexy*. I'm not. If I wear something slinky or unbutton my shirt a few buttons, everyone will think I'm a clown or a floozy."

Baloney! They'll be envious or else try to maneuver you into bed. You be the bold one for a change and watch the action.

Truly sexy people look the way they do because they

believe that they are good lovers, or because enough
people have tried to get into their pants. If you aren't
getting much positive feedback, you can't feel very sexy.
And if you don't feel sexy, you probably won't get
much positive feedback. Another classic, vicious cycle.

It's like not exercising because you don't have the
energy. Once you start, tough as it may be, it gets easier
and easier because suddenly, you do have the energy.
With all this new power turning your dormant body into
a dynamo, you suddenly have a real need to exert yourself. That's how a vicious cycle makes a full circle and
becomes positive.

The same holds true for sex appeal. If you push it at
first, the feedback will encourage you to keep at it. Even
if the earliest signs are only warmer smiles and heartier
hellos.

You'll be amazed how much courage this will give
you the next time. After a while, you won't have to *act*
sexy, you'll *be* sexy and it will show. And show it must if
you want to be noticed and pursued.

Speaking of what shows, your shape is an important
part of your sexual image — the way you see yourself
and the way others see you.

Many people don't feel desirable if they've put on a
few pounds. If you're one of those people remember
just because you don't look good to yourself that
doesn't mean you look bad to someone else.

I think we've grown increasingly fanatical about

slimness. Sure, fashion models are all slender and that's what women see most of the time. But why do so many women think that if they're not thin, men won't find them attractive? Check out the men's magazines, you won't find too many thin women.

Of course, thin women have the reverse hangup. They look at the Playboy centerfold and feel inadequate because they don't have big boobs. Most women secretly think that men really like the other type. What's the other type? Whatever they're not.

The truth is that different people like different types and some of us like a variety of shapes and sizes. Just because your body isn't the greatest, what makes you think someone else isn't fantasizing about it right now.

Men don't have to be tall and thin to be sexy and they don't have to be muscle bound jocks to satisfy a woman.

An interesting survey in Cosmopolitan magazine asked men: "What do women most admire when they first see a man?" They also asked women the same question. The men said: Chest, crotch and arms. Women said: The way he carries himself, his ass and his eyes. Which only goes to prove that the way we see ourselves has little to do with the way others see us.

A friend told me a story about a woman he was dating who felt that she was too heavy. Although she felt great to him, the woman was reluctant to let the love-making take it's natural course. Not because she didn't want it but because she was sure that if she took off her clothes it would be the beginning of the end.

After several weeks of ardent pleading she finally succumbed. To her surprise and delight, she was wrong. Contrary to her fears, he was overjoyed with what he discovered and he proved it.

As their relationship blossomed, she decided to go on a crash diet to make him even happier. Her love inspired an overwhelming desire to be thin and beautiful.

In spite of his protests, she was convinced that he was just being kind. She was wrong again. She lost the weight and lost him in the process. Her slender, new form did not appeal to him as much as her old, plump one, and her disregard for his opinions did not appeal to him at all. He couldn't believe that she had such a low opinion of her looks or his taste.

Assuming you don't like the way you look (even if others do) it is still important for you to please yourself. As long as you don't indulge in a neurotic quest for perfection.

Dieting alone isn't enough. Exercise is the key. And one of the best things about it is that you see improvement right away. An even greater reward will be your improved health and vitality.

Would you believe that a regular exercise program needn't take more than five minutes per day? If that sounds too easy, try two minutes of sit-ups, one minute of deep knee bends, one minute of push ups and one minute of running in place. Every day.

If you don't have the discipline, join a health club. Sometimes having spent the money, you feel obligated to get your moneysworth. Once you start, a better looking, healthier person will be all the incentive you need to continue. Your health, your looks and your resulting state of mind are priceless. So if you have to join a health club it's worth whatever it costs. And that energy I was talking about will be surging through your veins. Power that can convert into sexual energy at the drop of a handkerchief or a pair of undies.

Naturally, most active sports will do the same thing but most of us can't or don't participate with enough regularity. That's why daily exercise is so important. And if you can get your body tuned up, can your love life be far behind?

Trust Your Instincts
and Let Yourself Go

One of the most attractive qualities is abandon. The ability to let yourself go in such a natural, uninhibited way that you sweep everything and everyone along with you.

People who are secure about themselves have the power to let go. Perhaps if the rest of us let go more often, we would gain security and have a lot more fun along the way. When you can flow with the moment and follow your inspirations, sparks flash around you like signal lights. These signals attract attention and admiration.

Abandon communicates passion to most people and even if they don't consciously make the connection, they sense it. But most of us are reserved. We put out tentative feelers, we are afraid to paint in bold strokes because we fear rejection or looking foolish.

Not all your bold inspirations will pan out. And sometimes you may make a fool of yourself. But you'll also learn to laugh at yourself and that too will help you become a more appealing person.

Todd is a shy man with a stunning wife. I was curious how they met. He said it was the most impulsive thing he had ever done.

15

"It was at the Boat Show, a few years ago. Lots of people were milling around gawking at yachts and scantily clad hostesses. It was amazing that when I walked in this mad scene, I saw only her face. Mary was standing on a stair case looking at a display on the lower level. She was beautiful."

"It was a survival raft," she piped in. He smiled as he recalled his moment of daring. "I don't know what came over me, probably love, but I did something crazy. I walked right up to this gorgeous person and said something stupid like, 'Let's fly off together.' "

"Wasn't it Mexico or Martinique?" Mary asked, sipping her Irish coffee.

"I don't know but you said something funny about an aircraft carrier around the corner. The wild thing is that I wasn't kidding. There was something about her that made me want to take her away to someplace exotic. I don't know how I would have paid for it but I swear I would have left that instant if she had said, yes."

"Instead, we went rowing in Central Park and pretended we were on the Kon Tiki. Everything was so spontaneous and crazy it was beautiful," she remembered fondly.

Until you let go, you can't fall. Learn to let it happen without controlling your every act and emotion and you just might find yourself falling in love.

When you abandon yourself, you break through an important barrier. You are vulnerable and the other per-

16

son can see you more clearly. You make a quantum leap instead of inching ahead. By revealing yourself, you show trust as well as abandon and the object of your desire is more likely to make a similar commitment to you. If you go for broke and the other person doesn't respond, chances are they never will. This way you have an idea where you stand right away. So live those fantasies. Stop dreaming and start acting.

Sally and Bob began a wonderfully exciting romance by abandoning themselves on a cross-country flight. "I was flying to California and had a few drinks when I noticed this guy with big soft eyes sitting in the aisle seat across from me. Maybe is was the booze, maybe it was passion but as soon as we started talking, the sparks were flying as fast as our Boeing 707. I had never even necked on an airplane but within minutes, I was locked in a steamy embrace with a total stranger. He said he wanted to make love to me and I asked him where he was staying in Los Angeles. He said, 'I don't want to wait till then. I mean now. I've always dreamed about making love on a plane.'

"I didn't slap him in the face. I didn't say, 'Don't be ridiculous,' I just looked into those big brown eyes and said nothing. I guess he could read my thoughts because he took me by the hand and led me to the back of the plane. Soon we were both standing inside that little bathroom and then he was inside me. I had a skirt on so it was easy. The lovemaking was fast and furious but it was fantastic.

We lived his dream because I was swept away and I've never regretted it. The romance continued during my stay in California, then my vacation ended and I had to go back home to Boston. Since he lived in L.A. we parted friends and lovers. But we didn't say goodbye. We look each other up whenever he comes East or I get out to the Coast.

Lastly there's Mark, who was living in the country while teaching at a small college in Delaware. He knew Ginny only a few days when they took a stroll one sunny Sunday afternoon. They came upon a little pond in the middle of a lovely meadow. It took a lot of nerve for Mark to suggest that they take off their clothes and take a dip. But he did and they did. He didn't think, he just acted.

Mark's abandon transformed an ordinary stroll into a wildly passionate moment. It also launched a wonderful relationship.

He said at the time he felt so alive he just wanted to experience this one beautiful day. He didn't worry about the consequences of his outrageous request, he surrendered to his instincts and so did she.

If we all surrender from time to time, there will be many beautiful days to fill our lives.

Perhaps you recently came in contact with someone who sparked something deep inside you. Did you act on your feelings or did you come up with lots of reasons why you shouldn't? Reasons like: he looks like a mechanic, he probably never went to college. Or she's so beautiful, she wouldn't be interested in me, she's probably living with someone anyhow.

These attractions should not be taken lightly. More than likely, few members of the opposite sex have enough magnetism to force you to take them seriously. So when it happens, trust your feelings and act on them. Don't rationalize them away.

I've heard about powerful physical attractions before but Rick R. told me about an incredible encounter he had a few weeks ago. His reaction to a woman was so extreme he claimed, "I had to walk away or I might have died."

Rick started his amazing story by setting the scene in a furniture store where he was shopping for a desk.

"I saw this very attractive woman with short blond hair and one of those stretch dancing tops. She was pretty, not beautiful and her figure was delicious. I did something I don't usually do. I had to talk to her so I followed her to the lower level. As I walked down the stairs I realized she was behind me.

"We began talking at the bottom of the staircase and my heart started these strong palpitations. My throat constricted; I could hardly talk. My whole nervous system was going crazy. Even my legs were shaking. I swear to you, my head was out to here. My temples were throbbing and I got a severe headache, I was in such fucking pain."

It seemed inconceivable that this suave, laid back, successful man could possibly go ga ga like Scarlett O'Hara swooning away, overcome with passion.

"I had to leave," he continued, "I thought I would die. And to think, all we talked about was furniture."

"You should have at least asked for her phone number before you expired," I told him.

"She was telling me to go to Sloan's to find the desk I was looking for and I was afraid to go because I thought I would meet her again."

"What finally happened?" I asked.

"I risked my life a second time and went back to talk to her again. All I could do was be honest and explain that her presence somehow created a violent reaction in me. She became worried and flattered at the same time. She told me she would have thought it was a line except she could see I was really in pain. Then she added Nurse and Mother to her Love Goddess image and I calmed down enough to take her for a drink.

We've been going out for a few weeks now and I can only say it was worth risking my life."

If you have a preconceived notion of a Miss or Mr. Right and spend all your time looking for that perfect person, you may be passing up potential love and happiness elsewhere.

Lonnie S. had been chasing blondes for years. Lonnie is a lighting engineer who works on the set of films and commercials. He's a 29-year old cowboy with a long pony tail.

"It was because of Marilyn Monroe," he said. Claims he fell in love with her as a teenager and consciously or sub-consciously spent five or six years looking for a Marilyn of his own. He had lots of fun with look-alikes but never fell in love.

The call of the wild ended Lonnie's search. Her name is Okoona and she's an Eskimo. How many Eskimos do you know who look like Marilyn Monroe? Okoona isn't your typical Eskimo, however. She's a graduate of Fairbanks University with a grant to study archaeology at Berkeley.

They met at a party in L.A. Lonnie said he didn't exactly know what it was about her but he felt happy when he was near her. He couldn't imagine that he was seriously interested but gradually his feelings told him otherwise. "I was amazed to hear myself asking her out. Kidding around, she invited me over for whale steak and we both broke up."

The story has a Hollywood ending. They were married two years ago and he recently worked on the film "White Dawn" which was filmed in Alaska.

Okoona was nothing like the star of "Some Like It Hot" but she was special. And Lonnie was wise enough and brave enough to do something about it. Most of us don't.

How often have you felt drawn to someone at a party, or in the supermarket, or in line at the Zerox machine and done nothing about it?

These are magic moments and you shouldn't let them slip away. They're too valuable. It is hard to approach strangers and even harder to discard stereotype Princes and Princesses. But beautiful things don't come easy. If they did, we wouldn't treasure them the way we do.

Only The Real You Will Do

Have you ever been in a serious conversation without really knowing what you were talking about? Maybe sailing came up or one of Kurt Vonnegut's novels and you heard yourself trying to sound like an expert. You probably thought it would bring you closer to the other person and make them like you. If it is indicative of your basic attitude toward other people you'll end up regretting it.

It's hard enough to be yourself, it's nearly impossible to be the kind of person you *think* someone wants you to be. Often, it's embarrassing.

If he or she doesn't care for you as you are forget it and find someone who will. Appearing enthusiastic or informed when you're not just misleads everyone, including yourself because when you are found out, you'll lose a lot more than you gained that moment.

I don't know why so many people think that similar interests are the primary basis for a relationship. It helps but it's not a blueprint for success. Yet so many people grasp at coincidental straws.

She mentions Boston and you rack your brain to remember friends who went to school there. Maybe you visited Harvard one weekend and you try to stretch the experience into a semester. How do you know it wouldn't be more interesting for her to hear about your home town or almost anything else peculiar to you?

Some conversations can really become absurd when one or both parties try to link everything.

"Cheddar cheese! Oh yes, my Aunt Rita once knew a plumber who just loved cheddar cheese. He would kill for it. And you like it too, what a coincidence."

Have you ever heard someone affectionately say, "You're crazy"? Usually they mean you have a mind of your own, you're unique, you say and do different things. You're not always predictable. You're not me.

They're glad you are vital, alive, and entertaining. And because their lives are better having shared the experience.

Phyllis L. is a good example of what I mean. She could care less about fads and fashions, what's in and who's in. Phyllis is a chubby little charmer who does some modern dancing, designs jewelry and leather purses, wears long flowery skirts at all times, makes fun of herself, claims to be on a diet but loves to eat and talk, and redoes her apartment every six months, changing the color scheme from one extreme to another. Naturally, she does all the work herself.

You may know someone like Phyllis and if you do, you also know how lovable they can be. Whether you call it doing your own thing or being true to yourself, the person who tries to please himself and avoids hypocrisy like the plague tends to attract friends and lovers by the dozen.

You don't have to be crazy to be popular but being

the unique individual you are is an advantage, not something to be feared.

Sandy knew he had had his fill of Farah Fawcett look-alikes when he saw Phyllis. He watched in amazement as this little gypsy tried to sell her wares to the jewelry buyers of a large department store where Sandy is an assistant manager.

Sandy is your clean cut, square jawed Ivy League type and many of the women he knew were fashion plate mannequins. Most of them were salesgirls, buyers, or models and they all considered Sandy a prime catch.

Yet there he was gawking, amused and turned on by a woman who was not tall, svelte or particularly well dressed.

When he approached her she thought he was talking to someone else. Then she wasn't interested because he looked so straight. But a few minutes later she had to admit he was very good looking and his soft brown eyes were easy to get lost in.

Phyllis was bubbling with energy, good humor, creativity and a down to earth reality that made Sandy sense he met a real woman, at the least, a real challenge.

When he exclaimed how rare it was to meet someone who wasn't afraid to be alive, she asked him to lunch. The last I heard, they were living together and planning to open their own boutique.

The notice of being true to yourself doesn't only pertain to conversations. It applies to your total personality.

In a newly budding relationship, if one person goes along with every thing just to please the other, eventually there is a loss of respect, followed by a taking advantage period, then, too often, a goodbye.

Sometimes the goodbye is due to the agreeable party reverting back to their true personality. It can even happen after the act was so successful it resulted in marriage. My friend Burt didn't know that his wife had been playing a role till six months after the wedding. She had given such a good performance it was a very hard act to follow.

Burt told me she pretended to like Bluegrass music, (he was studying the banjo), camping, sloppy clothing, contemporary American art, Indian crafts, just about everything he was interested in. When he met her, he couldn't believe his good luck. The girl of his dreams had arrived at long last.

Once they were married she stopped pretending.

"We both loved each other, I don't doubt that," he said. "But how could I live with her after she suddenly changed her mind about most of the things that were important to me? It was like marrying a counterfeiter. I even tried to tell myself that she did it because she loved me but I still couldn't handle it. I didn't respect her after that."

Burt works in the Weather Department of a large Airport. Judy was studying dance when they met. It was love at first sight and it seemed wonderful when it happened. It's a real pity she pretended to be someone she wasn't, even for love. This may be an extreme example but it has the same sad ending of many new relationships. It just took them longer than most to find out.

You can save a lot of time and pain if you are true to yourself. Be the best you can be but be yourself. You will have to be loved as you are if you and your mate are both to be happy.

Playing the great pretender isn't an easy task. After the exhilaration of new love wears off, your false role will begin to grate on you till it becomes increasingly difficult to maintain.

Don't start falsifying your feelings or your personality. Instead make yourself so appealing that you are perfectly content to be yourself.

You Don't Have to Impress Someone To Make a Good Impression

Some people think every flaw will be held against them. To counteract these fears, they attempt to appear perfect.

This is a common phenomenon among singles and nothing could be a bigger mistake. It makes for wooden, joyless dates with people trying so hard to be perfect they can't relax and have a good time.

No one is perfect, so why pretend to be? The only thing worse than someone who insists on tearing himself down is the person who insists on telling you how great he/she is.

To err is human and to admit it makes people like you. The ability to laugh at yourself will make them like you even more.

When you meet someone, it's only natural to want to make a good impression. But that doesn't mean you should reel off a list of your accomplishments either. Sure they want to know about you and you should talk about your interests, travels, job, etc. but go out of your way to avoid one-upmanship contests or "Look how great I am" monologues.

More often than not, bragging (even if it's true) won't raise someone's estimation of you, it will usually lower it.

Consider this: *Even if your credentials are extremely impressive, it doesn't necessarily make you lovable.* And love is a much better foundation for a relationship than awe. Here's a good tip. People will be more impressed with you and like you a lot more if they find out about your exploits in a casual, off-hand way. Better still, if they experience your expertise without hearing about it at all.

Tom T. told me about a wonderful woman he met. She was sweet, unassuming, considerate, loving and feminine. Their romance began around Christmas and most of their dates were parties, dinners, movies and other indoor activities. He was really falling for this Mid-Western, old-fashioned gal.

As it turned out she was everything he said she was and a lot more. Another of his friends who happened to be a ski buff clued him in. His petite, 90-pound sweetheart happened to be a former member of the U.S. Ski Team. If that wasn't enough, an expert tennis player, swimmer, motorcycle and horseback rider as well.

Maybe she played it cool about her athletic ability. Perhaps the jock image had turned off other guys. Maybe a lot of things, but he was so impressed with this unassuming, woman that when he found out how remarkable she was he fell head over heels.

Men are particularly guilty of forcing good impressions. Maybe society has put too much pressure on them to excel. But you'd be amazed how many guys run through a list of how smart, successful and strong they are. Some even come out and say, "And I'm a great lover too."

Prove it instead of talking about it. Besides, bragging may spoil any chance you have to prove it.

I must have the world's worst sense of direction. Some people have a knack for always knowing how to get places, I have a knack for always getting lost. What amazes me is that 98% of the time, when it's a choice of right or left, I invariably pick the wrong way. I often say to myself, trust your instincts, then go the other way. This doesn't work either.

In real life, getting lost all the time can be very frustrating. But in conversation, it can be fun. It shows I don't take myself too seriously and people enjoy hearing about it.

I've also noticed that people enjoy stories about absentmindedness. Again, I am not really an absent minded person but we all do dumb things now and then. And talking about them seems to put people at ease.

My favorite example is the time I carried some dirty clothes into the bathroom with the intention of throwing them into the hamper. I'll never forget how carefully I raised the toilet seat, stared down and then tossed the clothes into the bowl. I'm not exactly proud of this incident but it is funny. And you'd be surprised how much more lovable it sounds than hearing how efficient I am.

People feel closer to you and more relaxed when they hear stories like these. In return, they usually begin revealing unusual incidents about themselves. Often these are amusing stories too and the shared intimacy works wonders.

This technique also has the opposite effect of parading your insecurities. Instead, it shows that you are confident enough to admit being the fool sometimes. A trait most people admire.

I would caution against making this into an obvious part of a routine. Everything works best when it is natural and appropriate. The important thing is to understand you're not perfect, no one expects you to be, so don't try. Sometimes your flaws can be your most lovable qualities. Right Ringo?

Jan W. told me about an otherwise nice guy who loved to talk about his physique. "He would describe his daily exercises, even how far he jogged everyday. He was really trying to tell me that he looked good with his clothes off and that he had lots of stamina in bed. I have eyes. If he looks that good I'm gonna see it whether he talks about it or not. If his intention was to get me into bed, he would have done a lot better with a few tender words and soft caresses. So what if he had a good body and every hair was in place, I didn't like him as a human being."

Not only won't someone love you for relating all your impressive talents, conquests, etc., it may turn them off.

If you want to talk about yourself, fine. There's nothing more frustrating than someone who keeps everything to themselves. Just try to avoid superlatives. There's a big difference between "I enjoy tennis" and "I'm a great tennis player."

32

Actions still speak louder than words. Even when there not perfect.

Let Yourself Be Loved

When your primary desire is to love and be loved, this chapter may, at first glance seem ironic. You're probably saying to yourself, "Here I am wanting nothing more than to be loved and this guy is telling me to let is happen. Fine. Great advice, only no one loves me."

Maybe there are some people who love but you don't notice because you don't love them. Even remotely.

There are many reasons you should begin to take notice and learn to accept their affection. I honestly feel that someone who can accept love from someone they are not turned on to will eventually become more lovable to those whom they find desirable.

This is one of the most difficult problems to overcome. I'm still working on it. For a long time, I prevented most people from getting close to me. I presented them with a nearly impenetrable, icy shield. From time to time, the shield would thaw and I'd seem passive or indifferent. On occasion, it would melt entirely and I'd seem friendly.

We all surround ourselves with walls at one time or another. Mine are constructed of shyness and fear of rejection. Of course, there are times when I simply am indifferent. I don't feel anything special for the other person, so I don't want to accept anything from them.

35

What I didn't realize was that love can grow when it is nourished like a seed that floats into our garden unnoticed. Care and tenderness suddenly cause the seed to grow, break the surface and burst into bloom.

Frank W. has the Kennedy charm and the same thick, shock of hair covering his forehead. Recently promoted to regional sales manager of a large oil company, Frank is 37, once married, and ready to settle down again. Only Frank has a tendency to cut himself off from people, especially if they are women.

He wanted desperately to fall in love but most women he met didn't live up to his standards and those who did usually intimidated him. One of the things that changed Frank's attitude was an offer to help coach the company's Girl Softball Team.

At first, it seemed like a silly idea but Frank decided to give it a try. He had never noticed half the women on the team even though he saw most of them five days a week. Because he was not attracted to them physically, he had never really spoken to them, except for business.

It is amazing how many of us associate with people every day, yet, never see them as human beings with the same problems and desires we have.

The softball team gave Frank some new perspectives. The stereotyped roles of sales manager and office worker dropped away and suddenly it was Frank and Pat and Suzie.

Frank's formality and indifference dissolved. He

learned to accept hugs, smiles and playful shoves from the women on the team. Frank found himself going out for drinks after the games and soon he began dating the second basewoman and the center fielder.

Frank became a livelier friendlier person at work and play. Instead of sitting home brooding, he was invited to home cooked dinners. He was learning to accept love and enjoy it.

Then Frank connected with Denise, a pitcher and executive secretary on one of the other teams. He had seen her at one of the previous games and was a little in awe of her long legs and blonde pony tail. But as he found out later, his friendliness and affection toward his teammates attracted Denise in a big way.

She actually approached him after their next game and told him so.

It took a radical change of structure to shake Frank loose from his barriers. Had he related to the women he worked with earlier, the dates, dinners and companionship would have made him a happier, more desirable and more confident man years ago.

This doesn't mean you should run out and join a tennis league, bowling league, softball or volleyball team, (though it's not a bad idea, especially if it's coed) but it does mean you should force yourself to be civil, friendly and approachable to as many people as possible during all business and social circumstances.

Frank admitted feeling love for several women on

the softball team after getting to know them as human beings and as individuals.

Frank had known Helene (second base) for years and had been aware of her interest in him but he never really talked to her because he type cast her as an over-weight switchboard operator. But during the games he found out she had a good sense of humor. He later discovered she was a great cook and a very passionate lover.

He says he was amazed that he enjoyed each date more than the last and now finds great contentment in her company.

His new found accessability and warmth led Frank to much more pleasure than he experienced as Mr. Cool and Indifferent. And I believe the changes in his personality helped him connect with Denise who was very much attracted to the joshing, hugging coach she saw across a crowded diamond.

At last count, Frank was letting himself be loved by Denise and Helen. He claims he is unable to make a choice and doesn't want to try.

We each have a much greater capacity for love than we appreciate. But it is buried so deep we forget it's there.

Most of us were raised on the concept that we fall in love once and stay married for life. That theory is about as real as Disneyland. Marriage, living together and living independently are all viable, lifestyles. Women no longer flock like lemmings into housewifery and men no longer look to industry as the only option. In fact, these days not all women aspire to being women and not all men aspire to being men. Many new and not so new combinations have surfaced and seem to be gaining in social acceptability.

Margaret Mead postulated that this growing acceptance of divorce, the single lifestyle, even homosexuality is an instinctual, social, survival mechanism due to over-population and the problems it causes.

I don't know where it's all heading but I do know that many loves are possible in one lifetime. Much more possible than just one love per person, per lifetime.

As single people, we should be well prepared for this new dawn. If it means there will be more love to go around, I'm glad to be alive, healthy and free.

Here's the plan: Let lots of people love you even if at first, you don't feel love for them.

Here's why: You can grow to love them as your heart responds to their love.

For a long time, I deluded myself into thinking that I didn't want people to love me because I didn't care about most of them. But as soon as I realized that they wanted to express their love, even Platonic love, I warmed to them and sooner or later basked in their glow. Lo and behold, love ripened where before a barren wasteland existed.

There are many kinds of love, of course, and we

both know the kind of true love we ultimately hope to find. Until you satisfy that wondrous dream, let yourself discover that intermediate loves, friendships, even kind affections can be a very pleasant state of affairs. No pun intended.

To love and be loved makes us feel alive and fulfilled. That's why we should do everything in our power to make it happen as often as possible.

Perhaps people have been misreading your cues. Or perhaps, they've interpreted your No Trespassing sign correctly. It's time to take down the fences, open up, and let them in. It doesn't have to be a lifetime commitment just a loving experience.

Accept love from others without guilt. There need not be strings and obligations unless you want them. Accept all love and you'll astound yourself. Discover that you have a far greater capacity than you ever imagined. Let it happen. Enjoy it. Indulge yourself.

Learn to love love and you'll soon be loved and in love.

Look For People Who Bring
Out the Best in You

The balance of our good and bad qualities influences
our self image. When there's more good we feel better
about ourselves. And the more we love ourselves, the
more lovable we are to others.

I have a tendency to be petty and vindictive. I'm not
proud of these qualities and it bothers me when they
rear their ugly heads. Unfortunately, I was married to a
woman who exhibited these same tendencies. For years,
we made each other miserable by trying to out petty the
other party.

I hated the stupid little arguments and balance sheets
of who did what to whom, but I found I couldn't avoid
them or rise above them. As I grew increasingly petty,
my self image kept shrinking. Being small to begin with
(5 ′7 ″, 135 pounds) I really began thinking of myself as a
small person both literally and figuratively. Acts of
courage, generosity and creativity were all overshadow-
ed by petty arguments. And that's what stuck.

Having learned the hard way, I scrupulously avoid
women, and men, for that matter, who bring out these
now dormant qualities. I learned that when you spend
time with warm, generous, loving people these traits are
brought out in you.

There is no doubt that these positive feelings affect

your lovemaking considerably. One area you always want the best in you brought out.

It seems that if I hold resentments toward the woman I am going to make love to, the quality of lovemaking diminishes proportionately. It doesn't last as long for one thing, and I find that I am less concerned with her satisfaction that I am with a woman who inspires loving feelings. When I am made to feel good and good about myself, it is immediately transferred to my penis, which in turn works overtime to return the favor.

Eddie M. is a very competitive lawyer who tries to win at everything, whether it's a game of gin rummy, a trivia contest, golf game or a simple matter like who is going to pick up the check. Eddie even brags that he's a better cook than most of the women he dates.

Like most of us, Eddie likes to associate with people like himself, so the atmosphere around him sizzles with competitive energy. And while Eddie always seems to go too far in his compulsive need to win, his good looks, loyalty and spunk stand him in good stead with his friends.

Eddie was in a vicious cycle. Most of the women he knew competed with him. When they showed natural weaknesses or lack of ability he grew tired of them. If they competed and won, as Robin did, he was disgusted and embarassed. Robin is a statuesque, female "jock" who excels at horseback riding, swimming, even baseball. Eddie was nuts about her for a while but he couldn't face losing to her, and she slowly disappeared from his life.

It had to happen and finally it did. Eddie met Liz, a loving woman who simply refused to compete because it was totally alien to her nature. In fact, she delighted in other people's victories.

This took Eddie completely off guard. Without his usual guidelines, he felt lost. But he had to see her out because, "Well, she's just wonderful."

He noticed a change that surprised him even more. Ed stopped trying to prove he was the best and started liking himself a lot more. He had been so competitive for so long, he assumed that proving you are top banana is the only way to earn love and respect, including your own.

While other women egged him on, turned him off, or lost interest, Liz brought out a gentleness that caused Eddie to feel better about himself.

He didn't really change. Few people can or should, but at least with Liz, Ed found qualities in himself he didn't know existed. It made Eddie very happy to see these aspects of himself come to the surface.

There is a song entitled "Hard Headed Woman" by Cat Stevens that impressed me years ago, and the essence of the lyrics have stayed with me.

"I've known a lot of fancy dancers,
the kind who waltz you round the floor.
But I'm looking for a hard headed woman,
Someone who's not like all the rest.
I'm looking for a hard headed woman,
Someone who'll make me do my best."

Drew is a very talented young man who hadn't fulfilled one tenth of his potential because it was so easy for
him to drift. And it was definitely too hard to write
songs or stories, seriously.

He could do both, as well as paint. Perhaps that was
part of the problem. But another part was sheer laziness
or maybe lack of confidence.

Drew moved to Los Angeles from New York, where
he had already released an album, acting as composer,
lead singer and guitarist for his group. The album never
went anywhere and neither did Drew. But wherever he
went, he usually had a woman caring for his needs.
Often, they were young and of the groupie variety —
glad to hang out, get stoned and ball. Few were demanding and those who were, weren't around very long.

In Los Angeles, Drew met Rona, a young photographer and part-time graphic artist. Rona is extremely
easy going about most things but because she was
serious about her creative talents and about Drews', she
pushed him to work at his music and his writing. She
also made distinctions between stoned time and work
time, something Drew hadn't thought about in years.

At first, Drew resented her and thought she was a
bore. He stopped seeing her for a while but she wouldn't
let go. That's when he knew she really cared about him
and that she was giving him good advice. Neither of
them had been earning very much money and Rona convinced Drew to join the wardrobe union with her.

Now she was really going too far. A job! But even

here, he gave in and did it her way. He knew he had to be in love. But he also knew they were both being highly productive in many areas.

All of a sudden money was coming into their little household, a funky back row apartment in LA. Drew had new songs written, Rona was designing the album cover and a screenplay was in the works.

Drew found a hard headed woman who made him do his best. She also made him love her even though he had to clear his brain and buckle down to do it.

Whether by "Hardheaded," Mr. Stevens meant stubborn, independent or supportive, the message is clear. Many people make a great show of friendship and love, people with the all right wrappings but not the best intentions.

A true friend will encourage what's best, not just what you want to hear. And they will bring out the best through their own example and through their love.

The fact that the singer was looking for someone who would "*make* him do his best" shows a lack of fortitude on his part. I would prefer someone who would *help* me do my best. But we all need different things and it's the end result that counts. If the best comes out and it makes us proud of ourselves it's bound to have a positive effect on our self esteem and our relationships.

Very often we look for partners in crime, so to speak — people with our same bad habits. We seek them out, to make us feel normal and take the onus off our evil deeds.

Heavy smokers and drinkers, for example, feel much more comfortable with mates who also exhibit these needs. But once they associate with people who don't smoke or drink they cut down, realize they feel better, and begin to grow healthy.

In addition to seeking out friends and lovers who bring out our good qualities or teach us new ones, we should strive to return the favor.

Being honest as well as encouraging is what friends are for. And friendship is a good first step to love.

Two important ways to recognize if someone is bringing out the best in you: 1) Your confidence level. 2) Your comfort level.

Bianca Jagger was quoted saying she was happier without Mick because he made her lose confidence in herself. Beware of people who want to pull you down or keep you under thumb. Look for people who want to bolster you, not flatter you.

How comfortable are you with your latest boy or girl friend? You can't force fit a situation. You should feel comfortable right away and that feeling should continue to grow. If it isn't, or doesn't, you shouldn't.

Do you laugh with them? Do you have good old fashioned fun? Do you feel happy? Or are you always trying to rationalize away the unhappiness gnawing away at you?

Determine what your mate's standards are, their upbringing and sense of responsibility. How do these jive with your own? Put aside appearances and good sex for a moment and consider the basics.

Are there qualities about this other person that complement your own and add to your strengths? Are you stronger as a unit or do you detract from each other? Can you learn from them? That goes from generosity to the theory of relativity.

Perhaps most importantly, can you learn about love from them?

If you can help someone else to be a better, happier and more successful human being, they are bound to love you. The trick is to help without nagging or manipulating them. And above all by being honest when it is constructive and shutting up when it is not.

If you can learn to do this, people will learn to love you.

Why do you think I'm writing this book?

Think Of A Date As A Friend
Instead Of A Date

One of the psychological barriers to dating is the mystique it creates about the other person — "your date."

There is a built-in formality; a date is an occasion. Etiquette, appearances, the uncertainty of how "your date" will react to what you say and do seems almost inevitable. We tend to grin and bear it, trying to make the best of an uncomfortable situation.

Here's a mental trick that will enable you to sidestep these traditional first date blues.

MAKE BELIEVE YOUR DATE IS ONE OF YOUR FRIENDS. You don't have to impress them, that's been taken care of years ago. So you can concentrate on making sure they have a good time.

Instead of being stiff and tentative, this attitude will automatically make you looser, funnier and more relaxed. In other words, more attractive.

I was first made aware of this technique by a disarming guy named Dennis, who must have developed it on the job. Dennis works for a consumer research company and has to call people all over the country. He finds out which toothpaste they use, magazines they read, people they admire. Perhaps when you've been hung up on often enough, after a while, you learn ways to make people talk to you, or you look for a new line of work.

Dennis and I became friends due to his exuberant good fellowship, as well as this amazing quality that made him seem like an old pal when we had just met.

When I asked Dennis how he did it, he smiled and revealed his theory: "It's pretty simple. I just treat people like old friends. Pretty soon, they are."

Dennis is small, has a mass of curly brown hair and a compact, muscular body. Sometimes his dark brown eyes contain a certain mischievous glint and he reminds me of a leprechaun. Maybe that's why he's been through two marriages and only recently turned 29. Women love him and so do men. He's so familiar and takes such liberties with everyone, you want to feel insulted but you have to laugh instead.

His special way of treating people can bring you phenomenal results. Dennis remembers his uptight years, especially after his first divorce.

"I think I took politeness and consideration to such heights, we would both be afraid to move. I remember one time I kept asking this nurse I took to dinner if each and everything was ok. You know, like, is this restaurant too crowded? Too smoky for you? How's the food? I noticed you buttoned your sweater, is the air conditioning too cold? And so on.

At the end of the date she told me she felt like a patient under the constant supervision of an entire team of doctors.

Dennis explained that now he is much looser and far more casual about dates. "You just have to stop worrying about insignificant details that get in the way. All anyone wants to do is have some fun and feel good about it. I do a lot less thinking now and act more on impulse."

When you act like an old friend, you strip away layers of pressure because you seem familiar even though you're not.

You've heard people say, "It seems like we've known each other for years." This is always meant as a compliment. It translates: you make me feel relaxed and comfortable.

Don't be overly sensitive about everything. When your date says something off the wall, don't analyze it and look for hidden meanings. With a friend you take it on face value, or laugh it off. Take the same tack with strangers and watch what happens.

If you treat your date like an old friend, you'll be more considerate and less competitive. You won't be as inclined to get into the You-Better-Reciprocate-Syndrome. With friends, we just aren't as selfish. We know they want us to be happy and if they don't seem to care at that very moment, they will soon.

Give your date the same benefit of the doubt you would give a friend. If ultimately you made a mistake, so what? You were a good sport., If you were right, you've probably gained a new friend.

Treating strangers like friends also lessens early sexual tensions. But don't worry, your date will still sense your interest if it's there.

The heavy pressure that often hangs in the air like a pregnant pause will float away. A symbolic way to do this and a very practical suggestion can be summed up by "A Walk and a Talk". This piece of wisdom comes from one of Eric Weber's other books. Instead of the usual uncomfortable seduction scene behind closed doors, try a stroll and a pleasant conversation.

"Let's go for a walk." This is exactly the kind of thing you would say to a pal because it's so unpretentious. It's also simple and safe because no one has to worry about making a pass or deflecting one. And if you want to be affectionate when you're outside, go right ahead. Hold his hand. Put your arm around her waist. It will probably be a lot easier for both of you because the bomb has been defused. No matter how excited you get, you know it can't go very far. At least not out there.

Treating someone like a friend creates other positive circumstances as well. We aren't overly critical of our friends. We overlook certain flaws because we see the whole person. On dates, we do the opposite. We tend to focus on petty imperfections as a defense mechanism to nullify our own.

We treat friends with respect. What a wonderful compliment to pay anyone. So what if everyone doesn't live up to your standards. At least give them a running start instead of putting them in cement sneakers.

We act as sounding boards to our friends. Even if we

don't really want to listen, we offer a sympathetic ear because it's important to them. For a change, try this with a date. Don't yak away about your problems, your achievements, your life. Sit back and listen, and act concerned even if you're not.

How many times have you tried to turn a date into a mate, lover, sex object or meal ticket? Substitute friend for any of the above and next time you'll be a lot closer to achieving your goal.

You're also going to make a whole lot of new friends along the way. So while you're looking for someone to love, you'll be surrounded by people to like. And that ain't bad.

Giving The Eye

If you can't look someone in the eye, either you're too shy or they don't interest you.

If you're too shy, let's do something about it. Eye contact is the next best thing to touching. So many of us are turned on by eyes, (the way they look, and the way they look at you), that it's worth serious consideration.

Cosmo did an interesting survey last year. They asked 30 men what women noticed about man when they gave him the once over. Most guys said, chest, crotch, and arms, in that order. Most women said slimness, the way he carries himself and his eyes.

Eyes were the first part of the male anatomy women saw. Surprisingly, the rear end was next.

Harry F. has big, brown eyes that look like melting chocolate and they can melt even the iciest of women. He had a way of gazing longingly into their eyes and they'd think, "He looks so loving and so easy to love." Exactly what he hoped they would think.

Harry happened to wear glasses. But when he took them off, the effect was like Clark Kent transforming himself into Superman. So you four eyes out there have a secret weapon, if you know how to use it.

Here's another secret weapon you may want to consider.

After many years of wearing glasses myself, I recently tried soft contact lenses. Take it from a guy who had problems putting eye drops in his eyes, these lenses are finally perfected. They are easy to wear and provide excellent vision. They also allow your eyes front line action without distorting fishbowls or metal rims getting in the way. It's pretty obvious that just about everyone looks better without glasses, so if you can afford to pay off the $200, it is worth looking into.

There are lots of effective ways to look at someone but the first and most important step is making contact.

Louise Y. an Oriental secretary in a San Francisco brokerage house is a very demure young lady. If she lived in China fifty years ago, she might be pictured covering her face with a fan while giggling and blushing. Louise had her eye on one of the executives, James S., and she managed to attract him without saying a word.

He went for coffee about the same time every morning that Louise would be at the Xerox machine. Several mornings, Louise watched him walk down the hall with his cup. She looked directly into his eyes for a split second, then quickly down at her work.

After three of these all too brief encounters, James was fascinated. At least, that's what he confessed to Louise over dinner that Friday. He told her she reminded him of a beautiful deer, staring deeply and innocently but ready to bound away at the first false move.

Louise, like most shy people finds it nearly impossible to speak to strangers. But she has learned that the language of the eyes can say a great deal without uttering a word.

If someone returns your eye contact, act on it. There is a very good chance they want you to talk to them. Anything will do, such as "Do you have the time?" or "Would you know where I can find the so and so?" Just say something to get it going.

Singles bars are an excellent place to use eye contact effectively. For one thing, the bars are often so crowded you can't always get close enough to the people you want to talk to. Fortunately, the eye conquers vast distances with the speed of light.

An excellent ploy is a wink. I was taken completely off guard by Nancy W. in a restaurant the other day. We were waiting in line for a table and we were each with two friends. I couldn't believe my eyes when this impish little pixie turned and winked at me. I couldn't help but smile and walk over to introduce myself. It was a very bold move on her part but it worked like a charm.

When a man winks, it is usually fun and friendly and will probably evoke a smile. When a woman winks, it is devastating and almost any man will do something about it.

A full, frontal, wide eyed, honest gaze is refreshing because you look open and interested. Hopefully, more interested in someone's mind than their body. Of course, if you are utterly consumed by lust, you won't be able to hide it. So try to tone it down. Passion is highly motivating as well as flattering. It is also frightening and usually has to be kept slightly under wraps.

57

Smiling eyes are wonderfully happy to see, sparkling eyes, misty eyes, an impish glance or an open honest gaze are all marvelous when they are directed your way.

The important thing is to look. Most people are too frightened or too shy. So those who aren't, have a definite advantage.

Moving this discussion of eye contact to a later phase in the relationship, consider looking deep into your lover's eyes during love making. Eric Fromm said many people are more comfortable getting into bed than having a discussion because in bed you can turn out the lights and not have to see the other person.

Can there actually be greater intimacy in social intercourse than physical intercourse?

Sometimes I just want to feel someone without looking at them. But I also know how wonderful it can be to look into someone's eyes while talking to them. It means a lot to the other person as well.

A very poignant moment in Neil Simon's "California Suite" came when a middle aged couple got into bed at the end of a very long evening and the wife begged her husband to keep his eyes open and look at her. "Tonight, let it be me," she implores.

I think it is significant to want to look into someone's eyes during love making. If you find it difficult, force yourself and see what happens. You may learn a lot about yourself and your relationship.

As another experiment, try to look into the eyes of everyone you talk to tomorrow. It's a very good way to make your presence felt and become more intimate with people, even if you don't want to fall in love with them.

Make Your Bedroom Your Living Room

Look at your bedroom as if you were seeing it for the first time. Or the way someone else sees it for the first time. What does is say about you?

Is it sensual, romantic, warm, happy, exotic, stimulating? Does your bedroom look like you are serious about loving? Are you?

If it doesn't, do something about it. Make your bedroom your living room and live in it when you're there. Perhaps you'll want to add some plants, or fur (pillows, throws, rugs), satin sheets, candles, soft lighting, erotic art (?) — all can help.

You are still the most important fixture but everything else can only enhance your lovemaking and possibly influence someone to stay for a long time.

I grant you that any two people, when the chemistry is right will be happy to make love on the floor or leaning against the wall if they have to but obviously this is rare.

Most of us need to feel comfortable, cozy and romantic. The more you can do to encourage these feelings the more you improve your chances for success.

Suzanne's bed had a lot to do with the inspiration for this chapter. I'm lying on it now. It's a beautiful four poster with a canopy top, but no canopy. Also, no Suzanne. She went to the store a few minutes ago.

This big old bed is an early American reproduction. She told me it was copied from a bed in a Vermont farmhouse, circa 1750. I liked the sound of that. The dark wood is stressed to make the bed look older than it is.

To my left is a wall of windows looking out on a courtyard which is ringed with brownstones and their little fenced in yards. Because the buildings are only five stories, you can see the sky through the big trees. When I awaken on a sunny morning I see strips of blue, gold and green through the narrow slits of the huge bamboo curtain which covers the windows.

On three of the windows she put together stained glass reproductions (from kits purchased at the Cloisters) and the vivid blues and reds look wonderful in bright light.

Plants hang from the ceiling in wicker baskets — lush ferns, and long, droopy twisters.

I just noticed a Moroccan dagger hanging in its carved silver sheath from one of the bed posts. It's strange but strangely beautiful and erotic.

The wall opposite the bed has a ledge which tops the radiator. I see it framed through the bed posts. There is an old wooden mirror with an inlaid design above it. On the ledge are a few more plants, a little brass chest, a Mayan sculpture, a fat yellow candle, half a dozen shells, a tiny topaz ashtray, a brass candle snuffer, a crystal rosebud vase and a brass incence burner.

The walls are white and bare except for a Picasso

bullfight scene, an eclectic room painted by Matisse (both reproductions of course) and a framed watercolor of sand dunes after a stormy sky.

To the right of the bed is an antique step table which she uses as a night table. It is mahogany with carved leather on each of the three steps. It was designed to hold a chamber pot which could have been used in the 18th century if one pulled out the middle step and lifted the lid. I wonder if anyone would use it today if the chamber pot was in there.

There is a bookcase in the room too. It holds quite a few books as well as photographs, a straw basket filled with assorted junk, and a bust by Michelangelo. He used his own face as the model for St. John.

A soft yellow corduroy chair with matching ottoman comes after the step table and bookcase on the same wall as the bed.

On the opposite wall, is a parsons table, stained dark brown, with a slate gray top. A Sony digital clock radio, green princess telephone and an electric typewriter rest neatly in line on the desk.

The small area left to the floor is covered with a woven Portugese rug which looks grey and green.

The far wall has a closet with sliding wooden door. To the left of the closet is a curved chest of drawers. A lamp made from a porcelain vase is on top of the chest. It was broken once, but glued together again like a jig saw puzzle with only one of its floral pieces missing.

Then comes the door which is interesting because it is slatted, so light shines through when it is closed.

Two not to be forgotten objects are a small sheepskin rug, haggled for in a bazaar in Marakesh and a brass Indian vase filled with dried eucalyptus leaves.

That's my love's bedroom. It's bright, warm and filled with things she loves and loves to use. Especially the bed, which I neglected to say was usually covered with either a fringed wool bedspread that's mostly mustard and orange, or a Moroccan blanket, also wool, which is blue, orange and white and is patterned with curious hot dog shapes. But she's not satisfied yet. In her never ending quest for coziness, she recently ordered a big fluffy, down comforter. Come winter I may never leave this bedroom. And I suspect that's the idea.

Everything in this bedroom and the entire apartment for that matter is here because it makes her happy. But there is no doubt that the intention is to create a very romantic atmosphere. I know it makes me feel romantic and that's half the battle. It also makes her feel romantic. That's the other half.

Clean Up Your Act

The expression "funky" is popular. It usually means hip, cool, off beat. It can mean very casual, sloppy or even dirty.

This look, whether it refers to personal appearance or interior decor is now "in", so it is being emulated by lots of folks.

Sometimes it is a studied funkiness. There are people who spend small fortunes on used clothing — pre-worn as opposed to pre-war is de rigeur these days. Fifty dollar jeans and denim jackets slept in by authentic Haight Ashbury and Greenwich Village hippies are considered prizes. Overalls and old flannel shirts discarded by farmers and their daughters are also desirable by many city slickers. Second hand furs and leathers are selling like hotcakes.

Before you get the wrong idea and think that I am totally against our funky friends, let me admit that it can be fun. It can also be imaginative and even beautiful. On the other hand, it can be repulsive.

As you know, some people have a flair for carrying off any style, no matter how extreme. They are extremely rare. If you have been tempted to use funkiness as a rationale for sloppiness, you are doing yourself a disservice.

I'm not referring to bumming around occasionally. Once in awhile it can be the greatest feeling to put on sloppy clothes, and to forget about shaving or brushing your hair. I have enjoyed many a happy hour in sleeveless undershirts, sunning myself on fire escapes and front stoops with a two day growth bristling on my face. I've known some women who let the hair grow under their arms and on their legs just for the sheer joy of it.

Let's talk about general cleanliness and your personal appearance. These are two of the most telling factors about you.

Without running off a litany of tv commercials for odors ranging from your mouth to your feet, and everyplace in between, ask yourself this basic question: "How do I smell?" In case you didn't know this is really the derivation of the term "funky."

It may win over a few people if you look funky but smelling funky is not usually a key to popularity. Especially if you are looking forward to an active sex life.

On occasion, I have enjoyed, and I've heard others say they enjoyed the smells that accompany lovemaking. The scent of musk and perspiration can be arousing. You will note that I mentioned smells that *accompany* lovemaking. If you smell that way to begin with you probably won't get as far as a kiss.

Naturally, I can't speak for everyone, but, I for one, am extremely aroused by a fresh, clean, tingling body. I can barely contain myself if a woman has just stepped from an oiled, perfumed bath. Or out of a shower, still damp and warm. Or all glistening and breathless from the ocean, a lake, or a crystal stream.

And I know that women feel the same way about

66

men. When I have run behind schedule I have had to greet visitors fresh from the shower still wearing a robe. I've been told later on that it was very appealing.

In spite of the fact that I am a Capricorn (The Goat) and goats are notorious garbage eaters (which I am with food) I draw the line with people. As much as I adore smooth, soft, succulent flesh, I really don't want to lick, kiss or bite it when it's dirty.

Of course if two people are madly in love or extremely horny, they will be passionate no matter what the circumstances. But this book is not dealing with exceptions as much as with general rules that can be helpful to most people under most circumstances.

Being fresh and clean is a turn on. To both of you. And as I mentioned, if you can manage to step out of a bath, shower or lake just when that certain someone arrives, the odds are definitely in your favor.

Sprucing up also shows that you care, that you are making an effort on their behalf. People appreciate this, it's flattering. It means you wanted to look good for them. Maybe it also meant you wanted to look good enough to excite them. Have you ever heard the expression, "You look good enough to eat"? Think about it.

Being well-groomed is also important for your head. It is an added bonus that it may make you look better. I'm referring now to how it makes you feel. And how those feelings are communicated to others.

There are some sunny mornings when I'll shower,

67

shave and shampoo (not necessarily in that order), get dressed in some spiffy duds and go out feeling like the sexiest guy in town. And whether or not anybody else agrees, I still feel great. And I know that this aura of sexiness and confidence is picked up by at least a few people. Many more than on those dreary days when I drag myself to work unshowered and sometimes unshaven. I just don't feel desirable and I'm probably not. You never know but that's how I feel.

Again, let's not go to extremes. It isn't necessary to become a fanatic about cleanliness either. It's no big deal if you have a blemish on your face, or a stain on your blouse, or if your hair doesn't wave right some days.

We're not supposed to be perfect. And attempting to look that way is usually scorned more often than not. People seem to resent it. Usually they want to mess you up a little. I've heard so many women say "He would look much sexier if everything wasn't in place," or "He looks plastic, why doesn't he loosen up?"

How about all the guys who have expressed a longing to see so and so mess up that perfect coiffure and let her hair down.

Casual tends to be more attractive than stiff, so don't worry if something is out of place. Isn't it a bore when someone keeps fixing their hair or tie or skirt all the time?

This is a mistake that I tend to make. I always want things in their proper place. Overall neatness probably counts in my favor but I know that I can go too far. Not only doesn't anyone else care, but they wonder why it's so important to me. I remember one woman saying to me, "You won't really be creative or sexy until you stop being so orderly." I think she was right too.

One reason people don't like this trait is because they sometimes feel unnecessary pressure to watch every little thing about themselves. They assume I am overly critical of them because I am overly critical of myself. And if anyone is to blame, it's probably me for being petty, instead of them for being human.

Getting back to cleanliness as a way to make you more desirable, don't make a fetish of it. Particularly when lovemaking has begun. It isn't really essential to rush into the bathroom as soon as you are finished. You can sleep that way, you can make love again, you can even revel in the scents and essences of your bodies.

When Audrey left her husband for about six months, she discovered that his mania for cleanliness was one of the problems. She told me that one of the things that most turned her on about her new lover was that he didn't feel compelled to clean up all the time. "He loves to make love when we're wet with passion. For some reason it makes me feel more womanly."

There are men and women who must wash their mouth out immediately after fellatio or cunilingus. They don't take into consideration that it may be insulting to their partners. I've also met some men and women who fear oral sex because of germs or because they consider it generally unclean.

There is almost no chance of this unless their lover hasn't washed lately or has unexpectedly come down with a severe case of hoof and mouth disease. Otherwise, they are depriving themselves and others of one of life's most wonderful sensations. And a beautiful way to express your love that is truly appreciated.

As far as a funky appearance goes, it may work for some people but these days, spruced up seems to go a lot farther with a wider variety of people. Why limit your chances if you don't have to go against the odds?

Believe it or not, suits and ties, dresses and heels are on the way back, if they've really ever been out.

In the sixties it was hip to dress down because most people were doing well financially. But the seventies brought tougher economic times and dressing down these days just makes you look poor rather than chic. Therefore, you might as well make the most of what you've got and well-groomed happens to be more flattering to more people. And if you're like most people, it will improve your looks as well as your self image.

And having your head on straight is even more important than a good haircut.

Don't Be Afraid To Ask

Some people have a tendency to be demanding, others to be so shy they think twice about asking the time of day. Neither attitude leads to popularity but there is a happy medium.

Diplomacy is tricky business. How direct you can be depends on what you have to say and how you say it. But too many of us do everything but ask directly for what we want.

For example, at the end of a lovely evening maybe you would like to go back to your date's apartment with hopes of further romance. You could be indirect and ask, "How have you furnished your apartment? I'd love to see it." You could be too direct and suggest, "Let's go back to your place and hop into bed." Or you could be honest and say, "I would love to go back to your place."

As a general rule, expressing your desires is better than hiding them. You may not get what you want simply because you asked for it but you stand a much better chance in the long run.

Alisha is a fashion co-ordinator at a plush Fifth Avenue boutique. She used to sit around waiting for romance to happen. Usually, it didn't. Alisha was infatuated with a handsome advertising executive she had been out with a few times but he didn't seem particularly interested in her. Occasionally she would call him and ask advice about different promotions she was planning and he would offer friendly suggestions.

Alisha loves the theater and sees as many Broadway shows as possible. One day she called her ad man and invited him to see "Pippin." He thought it was a great idea and admired her for asking. He was impressed with her boldness and felt flattered as well. He also appreciated the fact that she had put herself on the line for a possible rejection, something he had to experience all the time. Ladies, it's no fun but like a lot of things you get used to it.

So Alisha satisfied both of her passions with one phone call and a pair of orchestra tickets. (He paid for the dinner.) She took matters into her own hands and made things happen.

Don't be afraid to ask, it's as simple as that. Usually you have everything to gain and only a little ego to lose. Sometimes that's a gain too.

What you ask and how you ask for it are important but generally, a reasonable request asked politely and sincerely is responded to in kind.

Note: The subject of this book is how to find someone to love, not how to find someone to make love to. Please consider your requests in that light.

Don't Be Stingy With Your Love

Love is a precious commodity. And because it is, many people are reluctant to share it. They hoard their love the way a miser hoards his wealth. Granted, it is wrong to squander what is precious but sharing the wealth, or investing it wisely can make it worth even more.

Unlike a gold mine, our capacity for love is nearly limitless. So why keep it under lock and key? Instead of being a miser, become a philanthropist, at the very least, a wise investor. Don't be the farmer who saves his seeds for the perfect season, sow yours every season, always working to improve your harvest.

Instead of saving your love while you search for "that perfect person" create a loving environment that will attract him or her to you today. You may need different "perfect people" at different times in your life anyway. So be loving all the time and discover that there are many people you can love in one lifetime.

In other words, let those loving feelings loose. If you suppress them you just hurt yourself. If you express them, their very presence will make you feel good and will probably make someone else feel even better.

When you share beautiful things or beautiful feelings you maximize your own pleasure. If you have a painting and you share it with someone your feelings will be renewed through them. When you show off your city to a stranger, it makes you appreciate it all over again.

What prevents us from sharing our love? Ego. If we could transcend that fragile vanity we could all have a lot more fun and generally be more attractive human beings. But we are so hung up about rejection we become overly cautious about expressing honest emotions. We fear they will be misinterpreted, go unreciprocated or just be ignored. And maybe they will. That is still no reason to suppress them. Generating positive emotions is a reward unto itself. Expressing your love is much more satisfying than holding it back, pretending it isn't there or wondering what might have been. People crave to be loved and to hear the magic words, I love you.

If you are kind, romantic and affectionate, anyone you come in contact with will be impressed.

The example of Keith, Ira and Stephanie proves how well a loving nature can pay off in unexpected ways. Stephanie is an open, loving woman who is affectionate to just about everyone she likes. She was dating Ira for several months and though they seemed to have fun together, Ira took Stephanie for granted. One evening Ira invited Keith, an old college chum, to join them for dinner. He was in town on business.

The evening was amiable and Stephanie was as attentive and affectionate as usual. She is the type of woman who enjoys putting her arm around a man's neck or running her fingers through his hair whether they are alone or with friends.

Keith told Ira what a lucky guy he was. Ira said, "It's no big deal." As you might have guessed Stephanie and Ira did not last long as lovers but they did remain friends. Did Stephanie waste her affections? Far from it. Keith was so impressed with Stephanie, he asked Ira if he could see her when he returned to town. Ira had no objections and neither did Stephanie.

Over a candlelit dinner, Keith confessed that her loving nature created a need that he hadn't known existed. He told her when he went back home last time he tried to find a woman like her. Now he could stop looking for a copy because he had the original.

Stephanie was overwhelmed. But also delighted to be with someone who really seemed to appreciate her. His sincerity, which could have been a line but wasn't, made Stephanie even more demonstrative. Which made Keith very happy and very horny. And so on.

They now live together in Washington, D.C., where he works for a government conservation agency and Stephanie teaches fifth graders to read, write and love their fellow man.

The moral is this: keep on keepin on cause even if the object of your loving ways doesn't appreciate it, someone else may.

Let's say that starting tomorrow you go around with a more loving attitude. What happens if the first ten times you express these feelings you are turned down? Just tell yourself that you are perfecting your love for the eleventh try. For that wonderful person who deserves you and the best kind of love you can give them. Let them be the beneficiary of your experience and practice. Consider the other guinea pigs who helped you get the mistakes out of your system.

And if you don't succeed with the first ten, you don't fail either. Being considerate and loving benefits everyone, especially you.

Which doesn't mean you should become sweety milk-toast overnight. Or bestow something precious on every jerk in the world. Some people indiscriminately present sweetness and light to everyone. Much as the "Moonies" or other peculiar new spiritual cults. They are unreal. Something to avoid at all costs. Be real with your emotions and express them but don't manufacture them when you don't feel them.

Love and consideration do come natural, you just have to help them along; keep them in mind and feel for them. Then be demonstrative. Eventually, it's going to pay off.

How To Get Out of
A Dead End Romance

It is very common to fall out of love. People change and then, so do their relationships. The chemistry that brought you together is in a constant state of flux and the slightest shift can sometimes alter the balance enough to tip it.

There are many cycles in our lives. The need to be free followed by the need to settle down, followed by the need to be free again. Other more personal needs may also change.

At one time your lover may have provided precisely what you were looking for but after absorbing these qualities now you suddenly have a whole new set to satisfy.

There are many other reasons why a relationship can gradually or suddenly go wrong. But whatever the reasons, you sense it's over before you can admit it to yourself. Though it takes time for the sad reality to sink in, it is important to recognize it as soon as possible. And to confront your unhappiness and be honest about it. If there a problem that can be fixed, take a shot at fixing it. If the damage can't be restored, it's time to move on.

By being honest, should you meet in the future and feel a desire to start over, perhaps on a different basis, at least you are starting with a clean slate.

Too often I took what I now consider a cowardly, selfish approach to ending relationships. I wanted to cover my bases so I tried to find a new lover to take the other person's place before saying goodbye.

Unfortunately, many people live this way, even when they are married. They'll put out feelers, or have affairs and tell themselves it's just a fling. More often than not, it is a desire for love and a more fulfilling relationship. So they keep the one at home safely tucked away — an ace-in-the-hole in case the fling doesn't work out.

The most complex ending of a dead romance I've heard about involved two married couples.

Marshall and Toni came to New York from Iowa. He was well connected with a brokerage company with offices here and she was an editor at a small fashion magazine.

When I met them, Marshall would tell me how much he loved Toni. He also admitted that he might not have married her if they had stayed in Iowa but thought it was unfair to ask her to leave without asking her to be his wife.

They were in NYC for about one year (the fourth of their marriage) when Marshall grew bored with Toni and fell madly in love with a lawyer from Connecticut named Gretchen. She too was married and on the verge of splitting from an unhappy scene.

Their torrid romance went on for six months, mostly

at lunch time, till Marshall finally left his wife to prove his love for Gretchen.

It was hard for him and it was a nightmare for Toni who tried to hold on. She then moved out and eventually went back to Iowa where she found out about her husband's affair.

Meanwhile Gretchen was afraid to leave her husband because she still wasn't sure of Marshall. Her husband, who hadn't paid much interest before was now throwing tantrums and making all kinds of threats.

Marshall hung in there praying that love would conquer all and told me privately that if she didn't move in with him he would kill himself or go crazy.

Gretchen made promises and set dates but it didn't happen. Marshall was beginning to drive me crazy and I started praying with him. Finally it happened. She left her husband and moved from Connecticut into Manhattan. We were all overjoyed.

When they came home after dinner that same evening there was a message with the doorman. Gretchen's husband was in the hospital. He had taken an overdose of sleeping pills. I know this sounds like "As the World Turns" but it's all true.

Gretchen went back to her husband and when he recovered, she returned to Marshall. It was harrowing for all concerned. At last they settled into a semi-normal routine. Considering that their relationship to date involved clandestine meetings and splits with their respective mates. Now, nine months later a new couple was born and my friend Marshall was the happiest man on earth though he still had regrets about Toni.

Soon Gretchen shipped over some of her antique oak furniture and tried to blend it into Marshall's stark, ultra-modern Bauhaus apartment. New signs of trouble in paradise.

Things didn't match so well, including their personalities. There were differences of opinion, backgrounds and tastes. To make a very long story short, Marshall began having second thoughts. Only this time he wasn't worrying about how to get out of a bad marriage. He didn't threaten to go crazy or kill himself if Gretchen didn't move in with him. One year later, Marshall was telling me he would go crazy if Gretchen didn't move out.

He realized their romance was a dream and that they only used each other to get out of bad marriages. He still feels love for Toni and for Gretchen but knows now that neither woman is right for him.

Marshall and Gretchen tried to move out of one marriage and into another. It didn't work. It usually doesn't, even when the couples aren't married. People usually need time to clear their heads between serious relationships.

The motivation behind each move was supposed to be love but desperately latching onto another lover was a crutch that made their relationship unrealistic and unhealthy.

Fourteen months later the smoke has cleared and all the disentanglements were finally complete. In retrospect Marshall and Gretchen know they should have just left their respective mates and let it go at that. At least to begin with. But one often must live through a mess like theirs in order to know what to do the next time.

Because people fear being alone more than dealing with a bad relationship, they go on hurting the person they no longer love just for the sake of their own security, or should I say, insecurity.

It may be hard to believe but being alone can be much more satisfying than being with the wrong person. Once you begin to fall out of love, whether or not you are actively looking for a replacement, your partner will probably sense your unhappiness. People who love us are extraordinarily sensitive to our feelings and our changes. When this dissatisfaction is detected and we are confronted with it by our partners, we are likely to make excuses like business is bad or so and so really ticked me off, etc. At times we are not aware of the truth ourselves, or won't admit it.

It is so difficult to deal with the emotions that signal the end because every ending had a beginning filled with love and promise. And it is so heartbreaking to realize that suddenly they are gone. Instead, a bleak sense of failure hovers about us with a specterlike finality.

One of the reasons I changed my tactics for ending relationships was pure necessity. Once I realized it was going under I began to feel like a patient with a terminal illness. Rather than watch a slow painful death, I felt that ending it quickly was more humane. Either way is painful but now it seems more merciful and more loving to end it cleanly than to suffer through a lingering death.

Honesty and kindness are the only keywords to follow in these circumstances. And it is possible to be both. But please avoid rubbing in mistakes or bringing up trivial faults that will only torment the other person later on. As ironic as it may seem, you have to be even more loving than when you were in love.

Everything you can do to soften the parting should be done. But you must also remain realistic and end it without dangling false hopes when there are none. End it as friends who understand that love, affection and good times were a blessing you were lucky enough to enjoy. I know this is much easier said than done but you should still try.

Build up the other person's confidence, they'll need it. Praise them and remind them of the qualities that made them lovable to you. Remind them that there are other people to love, people who may be more appreciative and even more suitable than you were.

It is far less crushing to the rejected ego if you are not leaving for another lover. If you are this could be the one time to lie.

The best excuse is simply "change." We can all accept the fact that people change, circumstances and needs change. The world keeps spinning and so do we.

Not only is this usually the reason we fall out of love,
it is also one of the easiest to accept under these terrible
circumstances.

Maybe it is a cop out to put the blame on something
seemingly out of your control. But there is enough truth
to the notion to be acceptable. And at a time like this we
need what is believable without being unnecessarily
painful.

Rejection under the best of circumstances is tough,
under these conditions it is devastating. So be quick,
considerate, honest, kind and loving.

There is an alternative but it applies only to special
situations. Your romance may have stagnated because
you wish to see other people. Perhaps there is nothing
wrong with your relationship other than the feeling that
you are trapped.

If this is so, it is important to be out front about it.
Not everyone can handle this shift but it may turn out to
be a relief for both of you. If it's too painful for your
lover to allow you to see other people, end it and venture
out into the world alone.

On the other hand, if both are willing and able to
cope with this new system, your romance will be injected
with new life.

You may even discover that you really didn't want to
date other people but merely needed the reassurance
that you had your freedom if you wanted it.

The need to be free is a very powerful force but it is also a state of mind. What we must determine is whether we really want our freedom or the idea of it.

Put Yourself Into Circulation

Living in the suburbs or other remote areas presents added problems when you're trying to find someone to love. There are fewer people to meet and fewer places to meet them.

Clare is a recently divorced mother of two. She is thirty-two and learning about dating all over again. More practically, she is learning about dating for the first time, as an adult. Her situation is fairly common these days. She fell in love in college, got married and spent most of her life with one person, relatively sheltered from the social whirl.

As she expressed it, "Now I have to try to get back into the world. So many of us have led such sheltered lives, we are as naive as children. Being forced out on my own, I've had to relate to many kinds of people I might otherwise have ignored."

Like many women, Clare led a cloistered existence. Now, out of necessity, she has been pushed into business as well as social circles which are strange and frightening. Having to deal with these scenes has also forced Clare to gain confidence and sophistication in spite of herself. While her situation is extreme compared to most single people, there is also much in common with what many of us have to face. Her courage and some of what she learned may be constructive and heartening to those of you who are living through them today.

Here are some of Clare's experiences while trying to put herself back into circulation:

85

"I'm not a drinker, so going to singles bars makes me doubly uncomfortable. But it is one of the only places to meet men. Of course so many of them are married anyway. I had no idea married men fooled around so much. Up until now I had to get high on marijuana just to work up the courage to go into these places. I'm not aggressive like some of the women who go right up to these guys and start talking to them. They're all over them. I can't do that so I'm at a big disadvantage. After going to these bars the first few times, my ego felt this big. (She measured a one inch space with her thumb and forefinger). But after a couple of times I met a nice guy and that made up for all the aggravation.

Realistically that is what most women can expect. It takes time and quite a few butterflies in the stomach to work through the disappointments and insults, but when you get lucky and hit it right, it's amazing how fast the pain disappears.

Clare told me she also went to some meetings for Parents without Partners, some local community functions and political rallies in order to mix with members of the opposite sex. They were easier than the singles bars, she told me, but not as profitable.

It can be terrifying to be on your own after living in the privacy of your own neatly arranged world. Especially for a woman who has been isolated at home with her children. Men are generally pushed into the world to earn a living and so must learn to cope with strangers at an earlier age.

Clare began to do volunteer work with Abused

Children and is now taking courses toward a job on the Parole Board. She is also toying with the notion of getting a job in the city, mainly to be around more men. But she feels that her children are not old enough yet.

There is nothing I can say that will eliminate the fear of looking for a new mate or a new job which may lead to a new mate.

The rainbow at the end is a beautiful growth pattern you will discover about yourself. You'll see colors and shades of personality you didn't know existed. And if you did you probably thought they had long faded by now.

As you deal with the world, confronting it instead of hiding from it, a confidence grows slowly and painfully out of the fear and discomfort. Soon your experiences are more interesting and spontaneous. Vivid hues begin to shimmer where before a safe, steady beige surrounded you.

Once you begin to feel more comfortable with people and with your new self, you'll realize there's still a lot to learn about life, even at your advanced age. One day you'll understand that everyone you meet doesn't have to be a potential husband or wife. Then you can begin to appreciate a pleasant conversation for its own sake and perhaps, get a glimpse into another human being's unique personality.

You'll also discover that while we are all unique and special, we also seem to fit into generalized patterns and have faced many similar problems. And it sometimes can be very consoling to find out that someone else has already gone through what you're going through. It's nice to know you're not alone, and to benefit by someone else's experience, even if it's just the knowledge that someone else lived through it and survived.

Clare spoke of enjoying "rap sessions" with different groups of people — those dealing with community problems as well as personal problems. Sometimes they are called Encounter Groups. And she reinforced my understanding that conversation is the key to all relationships. Ultimately that is where it begins. And that is where it must begin for you. I know you were taught not to talk to strangers but that was years ago.

Begin a conversation with no ulterior motive other than making friendly contact with another person. If you are open and honest about yourself you will be surprised how much people will tell you. Everyone loves to tell their tale. A sage piece of advice on how to get almost anyone to talk to you: Ask them for advice. It works like a charm. People dote on being the expert.

Want to meet some new people quickly? Pick out a new "advisor" every day for one week. Choose places where you feel comfortable, whether it is a bar, a disco, your place of employment or the PTA. There are so many pleasant conversations you can have and so many helpful, interesting people waiting to talk to you. Just open your mouth and say, "Excuse me, can I ask your advice about something."

Here are a few other tips on putting yourself back into circulation:

Take a pottery course (especially if you're a guy), join a health club, take disco lessons and go dancing. Join a community center.

Take courses at a college in your neighborhood. How about a film course or creative writing?

Take tennis or ski lessons and join a sports circle.

Learn to play an instrument.

Jogging puts you into circulation so many ways, I'll let you think about them yourself.

Camping, hiking or biking are three more of your healthier ways to meet wholesome, physical people like yourself.

How about drawing, painting or sculpting classes?

Museums and bookstores are also good places to circulate. And who can forget the Supermarket or large department stores?

For many other helpful ways, I refer you to Eric Weber's *How to Pick up Girls* or *How to Pick up Men*.

The reason I began this list with pottery is because I met a wonderful woman while learning a wonderful art form. Both turned out to be soothing, satisfying and creative experiences.

Penny is a shy, quiet woman. She is not someone you would look at twice, especially as I saw her in a muddy, baggy sweatshirt and jeans.

She had studied pottery for a few years and was able to effortlessly create slender vases and perfect coffee mugs. I was the clutzy beginner and she showed a sympathetic concern, offering a few tips.

After three or four classes, she was more relaxed and agreed to have a drink after the workshop. A lovely relationship followed and we remained good friends for almost a year. She then moved to Ohio where she was going to teach physical therapy.

The main thing is to get out there and do something or lots of things. Being alone now, you can make decisions that benefit you alone. Pamper yourself and take a course in something you've always wanted to learn. Or get back to an activity you started and then had to drop because John or Mary wasn't interested.

Just don't sit back and wait. Confront life, put your arm around its shoulder and enjoy yourself.

Loose As a Goose

In the old days when someone said, she's loose, it meant she is promiscuous and it was intended as a slur. Today, it means spontaneous, playful and fun. It is meant as a high compliment.

Being loose can be a contagious turn on; it can help you and your date relax and enjoy yourselves; it can sweep you into the bedroom; and if you play your cards right, it can carry over into your lovemaking in a dramatically successful fashion.

If you've ever admired someone's casual, friendly, somewhat confident style, it probably added up to sex appeal. Maybe it was a flamboyant gesture they made or something silly they said that set off your fantasies. Whatever it was, it probably felt free, easy and natural and it made you want to be with them.

Why so many of us get absurdly uptight and formal when we are getting to know someone is a puzzlement. Yet, it happens to everyone, including me. You feel it coming on like a dark cloud and you don't know why but it seems unavoidable.

It isn't.

I watched a shy, frigid looking woman at a party recently. Several guys approached her because she was attractive in a Catherine Deneuve sort of way. Her coldness stopped most of them before they even got started.

A few more tried but acted so stiff it was painful. What's interesting about this woman is that she really wasn't trying to discourage everyone but her fear or shyness made it appear that way.

And that's why it was so gratifying to watch the transformation when Lou made his move. Lou wasn't the best looking man in the room by a long shot but he definitely was the most successful. It seemed so easy after he did it but how many of us would have had the imagination or the nerve. He tapped her on the shoulder and then kept hiding behind her back as she turned to see who it was. When she finally got a fix on him, as he spun and ducked, they were both laughing. At first, I thought he knew her but when I realized they were strangers, my admiration for the guy increased tenfold.

Her laughter was as much in relief as anything else and she was so happy to be having a good time, she beamed. Her coldness melted like candlewax and his looseness made it happen.

As the evening progressed, it was obvious that Louis' looseness was catching because she went from a stone wall to silly putty. Proving once again that it only takes the right person with the right attitude to work minor miracles. And no one is more thankful than the person who has been transformed.

I've always loved amusement parks. Carnival atmospheres turn me on and that includes the circus. Amusement parks are great because the rides are ridiculous, especially the scary ones. Just don't have a big meal beforehand and you'll be in good shape. Then if you can talk your date into accompanying you on the Cyclone or the Whirling Dervish, you're bound to have a wonderful time.

I don't know too much about primal scream techniques but I do know that going downhill on a roller coaster always makes me holler. I love the sensation of speed and having the perfect excuse to yell my head off. I always feel good afterwards and if my friends aren't nauseous, they feel happy too. If only because it's over.

One time I was so loose after several rides that I didn't pay close attention to what I was getting into. Fortunately, my date was a good sport.

The ride appeared to be an ordinary ferris wheel with free swinging cars. I didn't notice that the cars rotated all the way around as the wheel turned. And half the time you found yourself upside down. Not only was the ferris wheel turning but the screened-in cars as well.

We held on for dear life and I managed to control the swinging to a bare minimum by gripping the steering mechanism till my knuckles were white. As I said, she was a good sport and when it was finally over, we were both so loose we fell into each others arms for support as well as camaraderie.

Doing something daring and a bit wild is often what it takes. And I'm not just talking about roller coaster rides. You've got to create moments of fun and the more offbeat they are the better. Everyone wants to get out of their rut and they are thankful to anyone who pulls them out of it and out of themselves. I think most of us feel that way. We just need a little help to let the good times roll. Why shouldn't you be the one to initiate the action instead of waiting for them?

I mentioned that a loose style can sweep you into the bedroom. One motive may be as simple as curiosity. When people are very free and easy, it makes you wonder if they are that way in bed.

Another reason is that people who are loose tend to relax other people and this is almost as important as exciting them. In fact, the combination of looseness, excitement and relaxation are a devastating combination.

Lastly, if you can be free and easy, even silly, most people think you are confident. And most people find confidence very sexy. If you happen to appear that way before you get into the bedroom you stand a better chance of getting there.

Free spirited fun, confidence and a generally relaxed attitude can also carry over into your lovemaking. Because it is so contagious, you can succeed in making two people feel that way. And certainly the single most important ingredient for successful lovemaking is your frame of mind — your mental set. If you feel loose, relaxed and confident chances are you will be when it matters most.

In addition to all these wonderful reasons to loosen up, let me add one more. Charm. It is a rare commodity these days which makes it even more valuable. If you can add it to your other positive attributes, you are going to gain many points as a lovable character.

We all want to be loose and casual, the question is how. A rule of thumb might be "spontaneous silliness." Next time you feel a touch of craziness coming on, follow through, it will probably do you a world of good. If you're passing a playground and you feel enticed by the swings or seesaw, invite your date to join in. If you feel like bullfighting a taxicab as you hail it, do it. How about balancing on a wall or a curb as you walk along holding hands? Have you ever had the urge to bite someone's nose? Try it. What about piggy back rides, or sneaking food from someone's plate? Do a magic trick if you know one, even if it's dumb. Sometimes the dumber the better. Pick wildflowers and present your date with an impromptu bouquet. Here's a good one, dance when there's no music. Of course dancing when there is music is one of the best of all.

Inspire a mood of gaiety and spontaneity if you can. Which brings us back to trusting your instincts. If you follow your impulses, you'll automatically loosen up and probably have some fun. So will your date.

Don't Give Too Much Too Soon

It is possible to mess up a budding romance by going overboard in your exuberance. Whether or not you honestly feel love welling up inside, try to give these new feelings a chance to ripen.

It is a bit sad that these wonderful feelings you've kept bottled up for so long have to be released slowly, gradually and steadily instead of all at once. But many people just aren't ready to accept overwhelming passion so quickly. For lots of reasons.

Imagine the most wonderful perfume. A hint is intoxicating, a splash provocative but if the entire bottle is dumped at once, the effect is ruined.

Nick W. found out the hard way. Nick, in his late twenties, is an officer at a savings bank. Nora P. came in to open a checking account and they hit it off right away. Nick didn't waste any time, he made a date for that evening.

When he picked her up at her "Art Deco" studio apartment, it was as if he was seeing her for the first time. Her auburn hair was full and luxurious and her blouse was invitingly open. He couldn't believe his good fortune and told her so.

They had a lovely dinner at a nearby French restaurant and the evening was off to a splendid start. Nick learned that Nora was a window designer for a large department store which helped explain her somewhat flamboyant style of dress, at least by bankers' standards. But she was very easy to talk to and they both seemed to be having a good time.

The meal ended quite late so they walked back to her place and she invited him in. Once inside, she asked if he had any marijuana and he told her that he had some at his apartment. She said, "Lets' go," and he really knew luck was a lady tonight. Nick's luck held out through the first, second and third passion-filled evenings.

By now Nick was convinced he was in love and he began murmuring those three little words in her ear during their love making. It seemed to excite her but she didn't return the sentiment.

Nick tried to see her every night and when he found out she was going to be 25 that Friday, he planned something extravagant. He suspected that her family had money and intended to prove that he was her kind of people. To demonstrate his love, Nick booked a room at the Plaza Hotel and ordered expensive champagne to boot. By the time they got back to the hotel, he had already spent close to $100 on dinner and a chic discotheque.

The upshot of this beautiful, generous evening was that his lady-love got drunk at dinner, could hardly stand at the disco and when they got back to the hotel, she nonchalantly accepted the surprise, along with the champagne, which caused her to pass out.

That evening, one week after their first date, things

turned around for both of them. The more lavish his expressions of love, the more she took him for a love sick calf and an easy mark. The more blase she acted, the stupider and angrier he felt.

They tried to renew their passion the following week but the romance had already peaked. He put more demands on her time because he mistakenly thought she owed it to him. His hostile desperation eventually turned her off for good.

It is possible that this romance was doomed before it started. On the other hand, if Nick had played his cards right, he might have made it work.

On paper Nick and Nora seemed to have a lot going for them. It is rare that two people meet and fall so smoothly into a satisfying relationship in and out of bed. That is why the bud of romance must be carefully nurtured like a delicate hothouse plant.

Unless you've been on your own, you don't know the exhilaration of freedom or how reluctant someone may feel about giving it up.

Most of the people I knew lived with brothers and sisters, roomates, and then husbands or wives. If you went with someone in college, when you graduated, the plotted course pointed to marriage.

I was no exception. I even roomed with a fraternity buddy in graduate school. I had never been alone and didn't want to be.

Looking back, I realize now that fear of loneliness

was a strong motivation for my marriage. Like good children (she was 20, I was 22) we waited until she graduated from college, then tied the knot.

Freedom is frightening but it is also fortifying and probably the best way to find out about yourself. If it is possible, some of this independent spirit should be retained even after you fall in love and enter the realm of togetherness.

Before we jump the gun, let's consider a primary rule to help you achieve that elusive goal.

GIVE THE OTHER PERSON BREATHING ROOM.

Even if you aren't delighted with your mate's desire for independent activities, it's better to act as if you are. Make them feel good about their free time and they'll love you for it.

Best of all is to make yourself independent enough to enjoy the time yourself. That way you won't be acting when they want to do something without you. And the effect will be doubly positive.

They'll be happy because they are going off with your blessing instead of your guilt. Secondly, the same sort of desirability you gain by being independent, you also gain by encouraging their independence.

You'll probably have to work at developing this independence if it doesn't come natural but not only will it strengthen your relationships, it will make you a more stimulating and more attractive person.

Maybe that's why many people believe you have to learn to live with yourself before you can live with someone else.

Look at it this way, if your life appears full, you will seem more interesting and more attractive. Chances are they'll want to push some of that fullness aside to make room for them.

When you apply pressure, you can appear desperate even if you're not. This tends to frighten people and turn them off.

It may be a damn shame that you can't be as exuberant as you would like, but it's just too risky. There are so many conmen around that people may misinterpret your actions and think you just want to take advantage of them. Sometimes a display of overwhelming passion is just plain scary. And sometimes it may tempt them to take advantage of you. As certain countries do when they accept our foreign aid, then laugh at us and call us fools.

I hate to discourage you from expressing yourself, especially when there are some people who can graciously accept such gestures and love you for it. Unfortunately, it seems to be an unnecessary chance.

I remember giving Beth G. the bum's rush a few years ago and lousing up a potential love match. We also met in a bank; I passed her a deposit slip on the back of which I had written:

My name is Ken, I like you. Please fill in your

NAME

ADDRESS

PHONE NUMBER

To my surprise, she did. It amused her, she said. We had lunch at Trattoria and I was even more enticed when I saw the freckles on her buoyant bosom. (I'm a sucker for freckles, especially on chests). Soon I was unexpectedly dropping over at her apartment and making a general nuisance of myself. After several dates, we slept together but I had the distinct impression that she begrudgingly "gave herself" to me. All I knew was that I wanted more. I asked for dates every night. I promised that I would change plans I had made weeks in advance in order to accompany her and her friends to Vermont that weekend. I made lots of urgent phone calls. When the time came for our departure that Saturday morning, I learned from her roomate that Beth decided to leave the night before. I was mortified.

I blew it and I knew it. The truth of the matter is that I did feel desperate at that time and it showed. It also scared her away.

Now, I make every effort to keep my impetuosity camouflaged. It's not easy. In fact, it's damn hard but I keep telling myself, be cool Kenny boy, it's for the best.

One way I control my inclination for overwhelming enthusiasm is by asking people out for that same night instead of a week in advance. It makes me seem less anxious and it makes the occasion more spontaneous.

If you haven't been a reluctant suitor in the past, try to remember how the other person's reluctance affected you. It made them seem more interesting and more desirable didn't it.

Here's how Scott D. turned the tables on Margery L. and for once, ended up a winner.

Scott had always been Mr. Overboard — phone calls, flowers and declarations of love after three drinks. He also attempted to get every woman into bed instantly.

Scott met Marge late one Sunday night as he was parking on a very steep hill. He backed in at a precarious angle and couldn't move his Camaro without hitting the car next to him. Margery heard his curses of frustration and came to his rescue.

When Scott heard a voice say, "Can I help you?" and looked up to see a tall, tousled-haired blond, he answered: "You've got to be the prettiest good samaritan I've ever seen."

They soon discovered they lived next door to one another (buildings not apartments) and Scott invited Margery in for a drink. She accepted.

It seems Marge had just seen the play, "Streamers" and since Scott had also seen it, they talked into the wee hours, both obviously delighted to meet someone with whom they could communicate.

Scott The Impetuous had to make a pass before she left and she laughed it off with an "I'm not the type," and a kiss on the cheek.

Scott called a few days later and asked for a date that Friday. Margery was non-committal and said, "Let's talk about it Friday."

Scott didn't. He invited someone else over for dinner. When Margery called, he apologized saying, he had made other plans, not wanting to wait till the last minute and then ending up alone if she wasn't interested.

That Sunday Scott invited her over for a drink and detected an icy chill on the other end of the line. They argued out their misunderstanding and finally got together that evening. It was pleasant enough but reserved. They made another date which Margery subsequently broke saying, she changed her mind, let's cool it for a while. Instead of trying to overwhelm her, Scott cooled it to the point of not calling at all.

When they met several weeks later, outside their respective homes, he was curt and businesslike. She asked about his strange behavior. Scott told her he didn't like playing games and began walking off.

Margery called after him and said she was confused. He told her he cared about her right from the start, but she didn't seem to know whether she was coming or going. She said, "Let's try to be friends." He agreed.

They went to a movie and when the evening was over, he walked her home and shook her hand.

Several days later they met early, on their way to work and Scott suggested they go out that evening or the next. She said, "Tonight's no good, I'll call you tomorrow."

She never did.

Margery passed him in her car the following day and looked very guilty. Scott decided to forget about her.

Three weeks later she called and asked him to a movie. He was happy she still cared. They had a wonderful time dining in a little Japanese restaurant and never made it to the film. That night he kissed her once and took her home.

Sunday evening he stopped by for a visit and he could tell that she was ready. And now, so was he.

Scott had given her so much room he allowed Margery to make the moves when she was good and ready. She was grateful and she also respected his independence and patience.

In truth, he had given up on her but that was when the tide of battle turned. I'm not suggesting that you need a strategic battle plan or that he had one. But if Scott had taken his usual tack, he would have lost out a long time ago. The fact that he showed interest without pushing the sexuality too fast helped considerably. Because he gave her room to breathe, he was able to develop a relationship with the kind of woman he had always dreamed about.

105

Maybe there was a little too much game playing and a bit of honest confusion. Maybe he took a few chances. Maybe you have to.

Anyway, what's the rush? When a relationship is new you need time to let it develop in order to see it in its proper perspective. Since falling in love can be mind-boggling, give your mind a little time to unboggle before you do anything dumb.

Another aspect of the Too Much Too Soon Syndrome is that you may appear too easy and therefore unworthy of your prize. I'm not just referring to sexual mores either. Granted, not everyone feels this way anymore but be aware that enough of them still do. A high school mentality prevails in a surprising number of adults. Often it is better to let people work a little to win you over. The chase is usually exciting and some people feel cheated if they miss it.

Give them their money's worth but don't sell yourself short. No matter how terrific they seem to be don't let them think they are the greatest thing that ever happened to you. At least not right away. Time is the true test so make use of yours. A little distance will help you measure your own feelings as well as theirs.

One or two months makes a lot more sense than one or two weeks. If you are right about them, you'll still be right a couple of months from now. But if you rush it, you may never find out how right it might have been.

Love More Than One Person At A Time

You're probably asking yourself, is he kidding? Here I am looking for one person to love and he's suggesting that I love several people.

It may seem like a luxury to consider several lovers when most of us would be satisfied with one. But showing love for a few people just may be the key you need to help you find that special someone you want to love forever.

How do you start? Would it be too extreme to show love to every member of the opposite sex in your life? Imagine the look on your doorman's face when you give a big smile and a cheery hello instead of the usual mumbled greeting. What if you gave your secretary flowers for no special occasion? Would she think you were crazy or perhaps, in love?

To overflow with love and share it is a wonderful thing. And it tends to attract lovers like bears to honey. Try it in small doses, starting tomorrow. Look them all squarely in the face, smile and inquire about their lives. Maybe after a few tries, you may actually feel a little love. After that it gets easier and easier. And you'll be delighted to know this loving feeling is infectious. People pick up on it and find they want to return the favor.

Once your good fortune has begun, it is important not to smother your suitors. And this is one of the main advantages of having more than one person to love.

Very often when meeting new people, there is a tendency to crowd them. This is very flattering but most people want room to breathe. They want to make decisions about new relationships at their own pace.

When I've appeared anxious and pressing, it has turned off more women that it has attracted. I remember actually becoming a stage door johnny with an actress. It was exciting at first but I think it soon bored her. I was too easy.

Most people can tell if you are interested without getting the bum's rush. And this is where several lovers come in handy. You simply won't feel as pressured into making every new relationship work. People will appreciate this but they will also wonder why. And that will make you more desirable. The fact that you are seeing other people will make you more attractive to everyone, including yourself. Even if you don't tell them, they'll sense it. And that's one good reason why you don't have to mention it.

If you convey a sense of desperation, it will depress and frighten the object of your love. If you appear cool, independent and secure, it has the opposite effect. Having more than one lover can automatically give you this advantage.

This doesn't mean you should try to make people jealous or to brag about your popularity. It smacks of game playing and immaturity and can be the biggest turn off of all.

Keep your lovers to yourself and others will pick up

on it without being told. Flaunt it and it will only come back to haunt you.

I talked to a guy I met at a track in my neighborhood. Not a race track but a cinder track where joggers, ex-collegiate runners, and physical fitness freaks tend to congregate in the morning and early evening. Herb isn't the greatest looking guy — medium height, on the stocky side, glasses and droopy mustache but he had a nice easy style with women. And there were almost as many women running as men. I don't think they were running after each other, but who knows.

Herb always seemed to be laughing with one or another of the female runners and so I thought he'd be a good person to talk to. He was.

Herb is 26, unmarried and works in the stock market with ambitions of becoming another Bernard Baruch. And Herb has lots of girl friends. When I asked him why he has been successful with women he said, "It's because I know lots of them."

He explained that when he was younger, he tended to go after one at a time and put all his energies into the relationship. For whatever reasons, it usually didn't work and he found himself getting dumped left and right.

"I got fed up after a while and decided to spread the wealth around. Instead of concentrating on one person and trying to make it perfect, I just became more casual. I figured when it happens it happens. In the mean time I'm going to have some fun. That's about the size of it and I've been having fun for the last three years. I've learned a lot more about myself and women. And I'll tell you, I'm a lot more popular. I just try to be loving and considerate and I never hold one girl over the head of another. Now they seem to compete more for me."

One woman I know with quite a few male friends is a perfect example of how to ruin a good thing.

Faye is a twenty-eight year old divorcee whose two year marriage ended a few years ago. She is bright, outgoing and on her way to becoming a record producer. Aside from her engaging personality, Faye's popularity stems in part from her fantastic figure. She is only five feet tall but extremely voluptuous.

Her problem is not attracting men but holding on to them. The main reason for her difficulties is because Faye likes to talk to her men about her other men. It may enflame a few but it has turned off the ones she cared about most. She told me that she learned her lesson when her most promising romance ended abruptly, two weeks ago. He told her she had a big heart as well as a big mouth.

Showing your love without flaunting it is an excellent practice. It will help you become freer, and more magnetic. When all your eggs aren't in one basket, you can relax with yourself and express your individuality without worrying about every faux pas.

There is a tendency to become overly critical of yourself when you are trying hard to please one person. You second guess yourself too often. Will she think I'm not macho enough if I help her off with her coat? Will he think I'm too aggressive if I unbutton his shirt?

When you can stop worrying about every move and learn to go with the flow, you'll be at your best. It's just easier to be natural when the pressure is off.

You can depressurize your romances when you stop feeling that each new relationship is a do or die situation. Having several lovers makes it easier to feel this way.

If you are fortunate enough to feel love for several people, don't feel guilty and try to stifle it. Let your feelings overflow. It will heat up passions all around. Competition usually makes people try harder and it often brings out the best in them. Why shouldn't you be the beneficiary?

If you can stimulate this competition without ruffling too many feathers, you will find yourself in a most enviable position. And you'll find it a lot easier to find someone to love, who will want to love you back.

Massage Your Way Into Their Lives

It's as old as the hills and as tried and true. You've probably used variations on the theme as soon as you were able to get your hands on someone.

You gently massaged their fingers, or arm, shoulder, neck, hair, whatever. You may have gently massaged their mind as well. If you didn't, you missed an integral part of the plan. But this chapter really is about body massage.

Your regular, straight forward "Want a massage?" Massage. One of the greatest luxuries known to mankind and something we can all do to each other for free. Which is why few people refuse the offer and why you should never let the opportunity to give one, slip through your fingers.

A massage is an excellent way to become intimate with people you've just met. It is also a great way to get to know someone. "Would you like me to massage your neck, shoulder, etc. for you?" is one offer that can not be turned down.

By taking this approach you are showing your interest, consideration and physical affection. If your offer is accepted success is well within your grasp.

That's how powerful a good massage can be.

I have never read a book on massage, although there are many good ones. People who do read these books or who take courses in the Art of Massage (such as one given by Club Med) communicate at once that they know what they are doing. These people are instantly desirable friends.

Then there are the Orientals who learn about massaging the same way they learn about flower arranging. I'm not like any of these semi-pros but I still know how to give a good massage. And I think most everyone does. Instinctively.

Knowing what you like done (in the way of squeezing, fondling or stroking) to your own body gives you a leg up when you get your hands on your partners'. And that includes everything from their head to their toe.

Feet are two of the reasons I was inspired to write this chapter. My friend Ben recently described a foot massage he was fortunate to receive one beautiful, blissful evening. He was acting like it had changed his life, so I paid attention.

Ben had been playing racquet ball and was home relaxing when his doorbell rang. It was Marion, one of his neighbors. She had come to borrow his typewriter.

Ben and Marion had dated a few times but he had been content to remain friends, not being "too turned on" as he expressed it.

Ben is 34, wholesome looking and earns a good living selling office supplies. He stayed out of meaningful relationships of late because he isn't ready to get serious again, for a while. He had been living with someone for four years and it ended bitterly. Instead he'd rather play ball. And I mean that in the old sense. Ben is a jock and loves being out with the guys playing basketball, tennis, softball, whatever. At any rate, he hasn't let many women get close to him recently.

Marion figured out how. That evening Ben complained that his legs and feet ached from racquetball. Marion suggested a foot massage.

"It sounded a little kinky but it also seemed like a great idea. I was sitting there bare foot, just out of the shower, so I said, 'Sure, I could really use one.' Not that I ever had one before."

Marion assured him he was in for a real treat and went to work. A few words about Marion. She is a nice, Jewish woman who resembles Sandy Dennis playing a school teacher, which is what Marion does for a living. She is 27 and has never been married.

When Ben got to the play by play he could hardly control himself. "She pushed and squeezed every inch of my feet. Bent the arches back, pulled each toe, stretched the tendons, everything. My whole body felt great. That little tootsie did such a fantastic job on my tootsies, I had to return the favor. Only I offered her a complete rub down, which I happen to know something about. I don't have to tell you what happened. I didn't know she had it in her."

Most women have heard that the way to a man's heart is through his stomach. Marion may have found a new route.

A massage is a great way to make someone else feel good and an excellent way for you to make contact without appearing too forward. It can remind your partner, in case they've forgotten, how good it feels to have someone touch them in a loving way. And it allows you to express your feelings without having to say a word.

It may be hokey but it works.

I've noticed a funny thing about certain attitudes or phrases we consider cliches; they must have become cliches because so many people used them successfully and passed them along. With massages, it's word of hand. So to speak.

That's the other reason I decided to write this chapter. I was watching a tv movie in which Alan Arkin played a mute. It was so depressing I even preferred sitting alone in my room writing rather than watch the rest of the film. By the way, I really mean "MY ROOM". The one in my parent's home on Long Island where I spent my teenage youth reading *Tropic of Cancer* by flashlight and whenever possible, trying to give teenage girls massages.

What I was getting to about Alan Arkin the Mute was that he was very lonely. He lived in a boarding house with a family. Fortunately, one of the family was a lonely, slender, twenty year old girl.

When they were alone together you could feel his incredible frustration not being able to talk to her. Have you ever "dummied" up with someone you just met? Sometimes it can be extremely hard to get the words out. Imagine if you could never speak. But you could touch.

In a beautiful scene, she acts out a Beethoven symphony she plays on the phonograph. He is so moved he reaches out, touches her hands, holds them, then shakes them in loving gratitude.

It reminded me how important it is to touch (as well as feel). I had a new understanding how possible it is to communicate love through touch. Which leads us back to massage.

I know it works and if you think back you'll remember when a massage given to you changed your feelings about someone. Or other times, when giving a massage helped you along the road to love — smoothing out those rocky little bumps.

Since hearing Ben's story, I've exchanged foot massages and must confess it made my entire body feel as warm and happy as a summer morning at the seashore.

Maybe the ancient Chinese practitioners of acupuncture know something about our souls that we don't. At any rate, I loved every soothing, sensual minute of it.

I used a massage oil that I had in the house (not a bad item to have around). Along with the candlelight and soft music it was divine. Watching her eyes close in ecstasy, I wanted to make her truly ecstatic and immediately went to work massaging the rest of her sweet little body and vice versa.

Do you understand what I'm trying to tell you about the value of a massage?

Don't Settle For Good Sex

Sexual security is a trap because the comforting notion that you have a guaranteed orgasm waiting at the end of your evening can keep you from your real goal! Love. The magic ingredient that makes the difference between sexual satisfaction and sexual happiness.

Young people in particular, tend to confuse sexual longing with love. It is a natural state of confusion. When someone makes you feel that good, why shouldn't you feel "love" for them. You should but there is a difference. One is fucking, the other is love making. Both may feel good but while one is fleeting and often impersonal, the other is lasting and meaningful.

The pleasure of satisfying someone you love and vice versa is light years away from getting your rocks off. Today there is a lot of sex but a lot less feeling, meaning, passion or even fun. Orgiastic experiences are a common escape from loneliness.

Here's what Eric Fromm says about it in his excellent book, *The Art of Loving:* "Falling in love is a sudden experience that is short lived. The intimacy is primarily through sexual contact. Once past that, the closeness tends to be reduced. Soon one seeks love with a new person. A new stranger transformed into an intimate through the intense sexual experience."

Sexual desire may be stimulated by the need to

relieve a painful tension. It may also be stimulated by love. We have to learn to make the distinction.

To love means to commit oneself without guarantee, to give completely in the hope that your love will produce love in return. An interesting point is made by Rollo May in *Love and Will*. "People used to feel guilty if they had sex, today they feel guilty if they don't." He goes on to say, "The Victorians sought to have love without falling into sex. We Moderns seek to have sex without falling in love." In other words they repressed sex and were passionate, we repress passion and are sexual.

Machines go through the motions but never feel. In addition to giving physical pleasure we should also be concerned with giving feelings. Share your fantasies and your tenderness as well as your flesh.

Many people pride themselves on performance but are they really compensating for a lack of feeling? Sometimes we use sensuality to hide sensitivity. We are in flight from love and use sex to help us fly. Do you ever feel that it is easier to be in bed with your partner because you couldn't look them in the eye and talk to them? At least in bed you can close your eyes and then turn away and go to sleep when the sex is over.

Sex is so available it has become a pastime and a diversion. For many people it is also a way to avoid love rather than heading to it. When you fall into a new lover's arms is it the first step to falling in love, or is it another sexual conquest helping you to run away from it?

It is one thing to sow a few wild oats and experience different kinds of lovers but it is another story to become so preoccupied with new partners because you are afraid to commit yourself to one. That was the case with Frank and Donna until they overcame their neurotic patterns, let go and fell in love.

If there were ever two people who knew about sexual satisfaction without feeling satisfied it was Frank and Donna. Frank is what you would call a stud or sexual athlete. An ex-track star with a great track record in bed. He's a real macho character who took over his father's little construction company and built it into a big business. He is the classic tall, dark, handsome stereotype except that he is beginning to bald in back like Friar Tuck.

Frank was in his mid-thirties, never married and had everything to offer most women except genuine feeling. He was what is commonly known as a "sport fucker," getting it on left and right with any number of women any number of times then dropping them like hot potatoes without much explanation. The more women he screwed the easier it was for him to forget that he was still running. Running from feeling, tenderness and love. Occasionally he would slow down long enough to wonder how someone with such a full social life could feel so empty.

Put Frank on hold for a while, let's introduce Donna the Party Girl. Donna has three qualities that drive men wild: full, pouty lips, a great ass and a willingness to get it on that comes through loud and clear. Donna knows money, not that she ever has any but the good life is second nature to her.

She has dabbled in clothing boutiques, art galleries and antique jewelry but never stuck it out long enough in any field to make a success of it. That was her pattern for most things.

Donna's main ambition was to be seen at as many parties as possible, and have one orgasm after each. Her long range plans were to marry someone with plenty of money. She once confessed to me that she had been engaged to a rich, young playboy for over a month but hadn't made love to him. I was definitely surprised. When I questioned her she matter-of-factly explained "Oh he was gay."

"And you considered marrying him just because he had money?" I asked.

"Why not, we looked great together. Anyway we planned to have lovers and separate bedrooms."

She really didn't see anything wrong with that arrangement. Now she knows better. She's in love.

Inevitably The Sex Machine and The Party Girl had to meet. It happened quite naturally at a party in a photographer's studio. Neither of them knew the host. When their eyes met, they smoldered sparks flew. Frank and Donna left shortly and went at it hot and heavy for the rest of the weekend.

Frank expected to dump her, like always, because "I've got plenty of other fish to fry." Donna never planned to take him seriously, there were so many more parties. And he seemed to be doing well enough, but he still had to work. A dreary fact of life she considered bourgeois. But even the best laid plans . . . ah well.

They wanted to keep running but it was a little too difficult to pretend they didn't feel anything. Accepting this scared them at first. Then they stopped resisting and let it happen. Welcome emotions made the scene. Gentleness awakened after a long winter's hibernation, crept into the sunshine and stretched luxuriantly.

An inexplicable desire to give unselfishly made them feel like children discovering a new toy. This time they couldn't shrug off the intimacy. They couldn't turn their backs. Thankfully, they didn't want to. At last, "good sex" wasn't good enough. They sensed that there was more to it and for once accepted it.

Whether you're in the rut of running from love through sexual escapades, or the rut of steady, secure sex with an unloved and/or unloving partner, cheat yourself no more.

Either have the courage to give someone a real chance or if you've given them that chance and it doesn't pan out, have the courage to admit it and start fresh.

Love is the end of the rainbow. It's real. It's there. It's waiting. And it will change your life.

Don't Make The Same Mistake
87 Times

Are you self-destructive? Do you have a deep seeded desire to fail? Let's hope not. More likely, your mistakes and failures are the result of habit and the obstinacy to change.

Have you ever felt like an observer witnessing your own blunders? The same blunders you've watched yourself make eighty-seven times before.

You are face to face with an attractive stranger who is coming on strong. You've been there before and you can feel the faux pas coming like a head on collision. The car is spinning out of control and you aren't in the driver's seat. The scene unfolds in slow motion; you know what's going to happen but you can't stop it.

The stranger comes on in a taunting, flirtatious way and you tell yourself, "Be cool. Don't take offense, no one is criticizing you." You warn yourself to let it slide but "The Imp of the Perverse" (as Poe described it) is tickling your voice box. You hear the words forming in your mouth and you try to shut up but you can't. Out pops a nasty retort just like it did the other 86 times. The stranger leaves embarassed. You failed again.

How can we let ourselves make the same mistakes, when we realize it puts us in an unflattering light? It's one thing to be unaware of our errors but when we do know, there shouldn't be any excuses.

Vicky finally learned to break a negative pattern and now is living with a man who is glad to take good care of her.

Whether it's innate hospitality or insecurity, certain women have a tendency to over do the hostess routine. Vicky was guilty of playing this role to the hilt whether you were in her home or your own.

I certainly enjoy being catered to as much as any one, I also enjoy being a good host. During the time I dated Vicky, she wouldn't let me lift a finger. I knew this was a pattern because she had told me about life with her ex-husband. She complained, for example that he would send her to the store for more beer and dip during poker games with the boys. And she'd hop to it.

Her cloying desire to attend to my every comfort (Is it too hot, too cold, is the music too loud? etc.) finally got to me. I knew she had been on the losing end of several relationships and one day, I told her I thought I knew why. She asked for it.

Men want to respect a woman and it's hard to respect a doormat. And unfortunately, that was how her excessive consideration was being interpreted. It translated as desperation. And maybe it was.

By the time Vicky met Irwin she had wised up. Without becoming demanding, she laid down a few laws and discovered he liked her more for flexing her muscles.

She repressed the desire to do everything for him and found out he wanted to serve her from time to time.

They have since driven across the country together and set up housekeeping in Marina Del Rey where Vicky is being well taken care of by the first "considerate" man she has ever known.

Have you ever been on a date and for some reason beyond your control you found yourself apologizing for the lack of chicness of your suit or dress. You knew all the while you were making a mistake and that deep down you shouldn't be apologizing at all.

Your instincts were right. Remarks like these are poison to you, the person you're with, the relationship as a whole.

To be put down by someone else is usually annoying but while most of us are sensitive, we are poised enough to withstand a little barb and take it good naturedly. It is actually much more difficult to shake off the belittling comments some people make about themselves.

We all tend to be our own toughest critics but that doesn't mean new acquaintances (or old ones for that matter) want to hear about it. These negative comments have been the beginning and end of many a budding romance.

A close friend told me how disconcerting it was to have spent a wonderful evening with an attractive woman he was dating, only to have it ruined by a demeaning remark she made about herself.

"We had just seen Lina Wertmuller's brilliant film, *Seven Beauties*. In the taxi afterwards, I was sitting quietly, staggered by what I had just seen. Before I could say anything, she blurted out: "I bet you wish you were with someone intelligent, so you could discuss the movie."

"I tried to be kind," he said, "but I couldn't shake the sadness I felt. Because she had done it before, I began to wonder, what am I doing here with her?"

We all have problems, faults and occasional feelings of insecurity but we don't have to unveil them to people who are looking for reasons to like us. Let them draw their own conclusions. Maybe there's something about yourself that you absolutely hate. They might think it's simply smashing. Even your frizzy hair or the space between your teeth. So why spoil their illusion?

If you are less intelligent than your date, so what? The only thing wrong with it is revealing your low opinion of yourself.

The next time you feel one of those self-slurs coming on, shut your trap. Concentrate instead on your finer qualities. It was probably one of those qualities that attracted him or her in the first place.

Now it's time for you to break your negative patterns through a systematic application of will power. Are you ready to make the commitment?

First part of the system is to isolate one mistake you are going to eliminate from your repertoire of social booboos. Be very specific, define the problem in its simplest terms without any rationalizations. Such as, I will stop biting my nails when I am talking to someone.

128

Give yourself a deadline. Pick a day (one of the next 3) and an exact time. At that precise moment you must be convinced that for one solid week you will not permit yourself to make the same mistake again.

It's all up to you. And it is well within your power as long as you can convince yourself.. Not that *I've* convinced you but that *you know* in your mind and heart it is so and should be so.

You may have noticed my suggestion that you try this experiment for one week rather than forever. The reason is to show you that it can be done.

Too many people don't think they can't break bad habits even for one day. Of course they can but to them it seems impossible to break a pattern that may have existed for years.

So one week is all you'll need to prove to yourself that it can be done. After that you're over the hump and a new pattern can be established. If you wish it to. But first things first. Seven days from your chosen time.

But no excuses. No lapses. One solid week of abstention from whatever you've chosen.

Prove to yourself that you aren't a moral weakling. Allow no rationalizations. Simply don't do it. And it really is simple once you've made the decision to succeed.

No gradual withdrawals. A total halt on the day, hour and minute of your choosing within the next three days.

Participate in this experiment and discover the rewards of fortitude. And the satisfaction of knowing that you are taking positive steps to become a more desirable, lovable person.

Do you think I want to be sitting here writing this book now. Of course I don't but I have to. I write at the same time every week and I don't vary come rain or shine because without the structure and discipline I know I won't do it. I'm lazy, you know. But I know that as hard as it is now, I'll be proud of myself when I finish. And so will you.

Where There's Hate
There May Be Love

Have you ever felt an irrational, intense dislike for someone without being able to put your finger on it? Maybe you've experienced the reverse: feeling hated by someone without knowing why.

Either way, you might have wondered where all this energy came from and why it was being generated. I suspect that it is a key to deep feelings rather than superficial ones. Generally, when that much interest is directed toward another person it is an indication that beneath the surface anger there is the pain of love.

There are times when people hate one another because they have worked out a scenario of rejection in their minds without ever trying to make it work. They have decided that they will be laughed at and turned down or else toyed with and tossed aside. And so they hate you (or you them) because of an unrequited love that was never experienced except in Fantasyland.

There is another version. In this plot the hurt was not totally imagined but triggered by some event. Perhaps someone did inadvertently insult the other person. If the insultee was previously infatuated with the insulter, chances are the situation may be blown out of all proportion.

We are all so fragile and sensitive, especially when it comes to love and ego that the slightest ruffle of our feathers and our beaks and claws are quickly exposed.

From now on you should be on the lookout for passionate dislike, simply because it's passionate. If you feel it directed toward a specific person analyze it. Have you concocted petty reasons to justify your hatred in order to mask what you really feel? If so, shouldn't you try to overcome this childish display of temper and do something constructive? Like give them another chance instead of fueling what may start out as a one sided battle and develop into a full scale war with legitimate animosity on both sides.

Think what impact a display of kindness could have coming from a so called "enemy." This unexpected change of attitude will be suspect at first but if you follow up with a second dose, you can turn the tables quite dramatically. Signs of friendship will definitely make a deeper impression coming from you than they would coming from someone who has always been friendly.

It's never too late to turn one of these seemingly hopeless messes into a potential love but it takes patience, honesty and love to make it happen. Now I am not by any means suggesting that you go out of your way to alienate someone just so you can do an about face for the sake of making a big impression. But I am saying that if you can admit to yourself that the reason you "hate" someone is because you don't think they will ever love you, take a shot at proving yourself wrong. If I'm wrong, you can always go back to hating. You can even hate me if you really want to waste your energy.

Being the hated one may be an even better stroke of luck because if you play your cards right you will be the loved one before long. I have been amazed to hear women say things like, "I wouldn't touch you with a ten foot pole" or "Never in a million years would I get it on with you" only to find myself deeply embroiled with these same protesters weeks or months later. I always used to believe these kind of statements before and they hurt, until I learned that no situation is as bleak as it seems.

So many relationships begin out of casual interest, general boredom or loneliness that if you can redirect the intensity of your anger you can create a romance born of passion.

I observed my brother and his girlfriend playing together one afternoon. She would pinch, bite or hit him from time to time in order to provoke him or get his attention. It was all very playful. Over the same weekend, I brought a snowball into their house and splattered him with it. He laughed and explained to another guest, "That's how we show our affection." Sometimes it is a lot easier to express your love by fussin'n fightin than by sweetness. How many times have you used symbolic snowballs, pinches or punches as a general approach to life and love? It may not be the best way but it is one way and we should learn to recognize it and use it to our best advantage when appropriate.

If you can be aware of it when it is directed at you, you may learn to feel flattered instead of being offended.

Paul's romance with Belinda is the classic example of this sort of turn about from hate to love. For several years they were like cats and dogs who hissed and barked whenever they bumped into each other around the office. They both worked for a large textile company.

He had his reasons for disliking her. She was haughty, indifferent and too cool — a pattern designer who always wore the hippest clothes. And to top it off, she was a militant women's libber.

Belinda disliked Paul for being sarcastic, good looking and generally obnoxious. In addition she considered him a heartbreaker who preyed upon sweet, simple secretaries.

With all this excellent ammunition, they went about bickering and sniping, or feigning indifference and pretending to ignore each other. All the while their hearts were smoldering with desire instead of hatred. One year later, the coals were finally fanned into flame.

It happened when circumstance brought them into closer proximity than the confines of their work. It was over a weekend in the Hamptons at one of those beach houses shared by a dozen people who all invite friends. They found themselves houseguests among many strangers.

Maybe it was the change of locale. Maybe it was because they were alone. Maybe it was because they were like poles of the magnet sometimes attracting, sometimes repelling. Whatever it was, they let their guard down and discovered what they secretly suspected: that they liked, respected and desired each other.

Paul waited for a gesture from Belinda and she waited for a sign from him. It turned out to be a near-simultaneous offer to make a drink for the other followed by shy laughter and a melting of their respective icebergs.

It was a long awaited moment that was welcomed with the relief that honesty always brings. Especially self-honesty. And the pleasure of undoing all the bad feelings that had been built up. At last they could enjoy what they really felt even if they felt they were walking on eggshells. Once they suspected that the other was going through the exact same insecurities, they stopped worrying about the eggshells and made a wonderful souffle.

When You Least Expect It

I don't know how many times I've heard the expression, "You'll meet someone when you least expect it," or "You'll fall in love when you're not looking for it."

If at first this philosophy seems to run contrary to the basic guidelines already laid down, be patient. When I lived through the experience, I understood what everyone was talking about. Analyzing the event, I realize that what happened was not really inconsistent with the other ideas in this book.

Thus far I have preached positive action rather than sitting back in the hopes that lightning (in the form of love) will strike; so you may very well ask, "How can I make a conscious effort to find a lover when I'm not looking?"

It's a matter of degree as well as a state of mind.

Maybe it boils down to not trying so hard, all the time. Being ready, of course, sending out positive energy waves but also living your life to the fullest without focusing all your efforts on finding a lover.

Sometimes, it may take a change of tactics like going to the other extreme. Instead of constantly spinning webs to snare the next nice looking person who turns the corner, just go about your business without being so obvious. Taken on another level: live your life, from time to time, without making a conscious effort to look at all.

137

Ah hah! But what about the subconscious? That will always be working for you and it just may be the most effective drawing card of all. Putting together all your positive energies and appeals, then sublimating them and projecting them from within, you're well armed but not hunting. You are a self-centered, independent, sexy, loving nucleus just waiting to connect. So just leave it there for a while, smoldering under the surface, ready to ignite with the proper spark.

Even when you least expect it.

Here's how it happened to me. I really was not aware of falling in love more often when I was looking or when I wasn't looking. To be honest, I didn't think about it. If I had, I would have thought, I'm always looking.

There was a period of several months when I had terminated a relationship that had dragged on for too long and I was feeling blue about it. I dated some long standing girl friends who I could enjoy but with whom I had long ago determined would never be serious lovers.

It was Spring and I was heavily on the prowl for a new love, hopeful as the buds on the trees in Central Park. I searched hither and yon, making drastic efforts to talk to new people, swimming, dieting and playing tennis so I would look healthy, active and suntanned. But alas, all to no avail.

I met a few good possibilites but things never clicked and I had to let them drop by the wayside. I went back to the old, familiar standbys and resolved to have some fun, which I did. But fun is not ecstacy.

All of a sudden, it was summer. I had planned to spend the month of July at my parents' home on Long Island. I wanted to get out of the city, save a little money and isolate myself, so I could devote more time to this book.

I geared down for more work and less play. Not easy in the summer but I did a pretty good job of psyching myself into it. There I was, commuting on the Long Island Railroad, mentally prepared for a solid month of the good old Puritan work ethic with an occasional overnight fling in the city to make life bearable.

One week went by, one and a half weeks went by. I made a date to stay in the city that Wednesday night but at the last minute, my date couldn't make it. Oh well, you can always work on the book. "A fine thing" I thought, "here I am writing a book about how to find someone to love and I'm left high, dry and lonesome. It's not only unfair, it isn't logical, as Spock would say. Well . . . I'll just go out alone, eat dinner alone and work on this damn book."

That's what I was thinking as I sat on the steps of my brownstone watching the sun set across the Hudson river, sinking slowly into the Garden state on the other side. Then I saw her walking up the street with the last golden rays of daylight shimmering in her hair. I looked at her, she looked at me, then she walked up the stairs of the building next to mine.

"Who's the lucky guy she's visiting?" I wondered. As I bit my lower lip she came out and asked me if I lived here. It seems she was just moving in, and had come by to pick up keys from the superintendent, who also happened to be the super for my building.

I explained that Mrs. P, our ever reliable Islandic super, usually kept her word and if she said she would be here at 6:30, I was certain she would be here momentarily, etc. I also volunteered my telephone if she wanted to call and check. Perhaps Mrs. P was sleeping or out back with her cats.

Upstairs Marla told me she had just moved from California and this was going to be her first apartment in the Big City. We liked each other already and enjoyed this chance meeting. When the super returned ten minutes later I took her next door to pick up her keys and she invited me to walk up the five flights to her brand new, furnitureless, studio apartment with a terrace that looked into the same lovely courtyard I faced next door.

I then invited her to dinner but she declined, explaining that her brother expected her back in Brooklyn where she was living temporarily. But she promised to get together the following week after she was moved in. And she did. And we did. Things were blossoming beautifully but there appeared to be a hitch on the horizon.

I met someone else, quite by accident, sort of. It was lunch hour and a friend and I decided to see "Star Wars," a science fiction fantasy that was fast becoming the summer block buster. I had already seen the film and enjoyed it tremendously but my friend hadn't though he had tried a few times.

It was a rainy Monday and we both need some cheering up.

As I exited the elevator in our office building and entered the lobby, I accidentally stumbled into my friend because I wasn't watching where I was walking. I was watching a lovely woman with a big smile, a sweetly rounded tank top and a flowing peasant dress.

I apologized for my clumsiness; he understood having seen me see her. We went outside to look for a taxi in the rain, no easy task. I don't know how it happened but here she was again, on the sidewalk next to me, her green eyes twinkling under her floral umbrella.

When I am inspired, I manage to sneak past my basic shyness, open my mouth, and speak to certain lovely strangers. "Have you seen Star Wars?" I heard myself say. "Why, no" she beamed. I thought I detected a drawl. I invited her to join us and Oh Happy Day, to my amazement, she accepted.

In the taxi we talked a little, during the movie we talked a little more, and afterwards, when my friend kindly split for work, we agreed to get together the following week for lunch.

The following Monday she called to say she was in the building could she stop by. We were off and running. A stroll through the UN gardens (the roses are still in bloom in July), then a secluded bench for two in the Anna Roosevelt Memorial garden.

Suddenly, quite unexpectedly, with no plans aforethought, lightning struck twice in the same spot, my heart. Both romances continued to grow till I settled into a groove with the Southern Belle.

No sooner had I given up hope of finding even one when Shazam! my hands and heart were full.

How unexpectedly lucky can a person get? I sure hope you find out. Maybe it will happen when you're not pushing so hard. Maybe that's why it happens. If all your concentrated efforts have come to no avail lately, ease up. And watch out for lightning.

Compromise and Perseverance

This is a tough chapter to write and it will probably be a tough one to read. It deals with a reality that is much easier said than done. It has to do with being fair, with giving as well as receiving, with losing a few as well as winning a few.

An editorial I read recently discussed the vast numbers of single people living in this country, twice as many as during the sixties. The article stated that "freedom and independence" were the reasons given by singles for their chosen lifestyle. The journalist observed that "selfishness and self-indulgence" were more likely explanations. Since this point of view came from an editorial it is opinion rather than fact, yet, it made me wonder.

Being single certainly can foster self-indulgence. And for many people, this pattern can all too easily become a way of life. It is also possible that people who are inclined to be self-indulgent are more likely to be single. Either way, this attitude may be the prevailing one for many single people.

When you are committed primarily to pleasing yourself, it is much simpler to dump your partner at the first sign of a hassle rather than to try and work it out. Why bother, you may say, there are lots of other fish in the sea. This is true, of course, but what you really have to decide is whether you want to remain a single entity or evolve into a twosome.

A certain amount of self-love and self-indulgence is both healthy and necessary but not to the exclusion of others.

Learning to share is one of childhood's most difficult lessons. Some people take most of their lives to learn it. My kid brother isn't one of them. He's a quick study. Maybe it comes from being born second.

I was talking to him a while ago and asked what he felt was the key to his two successful relationships. He thought for a moment, then said, "Compromise and perseverance."

Thus far, Robbie has had a couple of serious romances. The first lasted four years, his latest is going strong after two. My brother is 28, has never married and seems in no hurry to change that situation (It changed May 30, 1978 when he married number two.)

The two women in his life couldn't be more different. He worked hard to be fair to both of them and to adjust to their contrasting temperaments and idiosyncracies.

The first is a small, delicate, intellectual from a well-to-do Jewish family. They met at college. The second is a buxom Christian outdoorswoman who has been foot-loose and fancy-free ever since she was 17 because her parents never had much money. They met while on vacation in Lake Tahoe. Both women gave him what he needed at the time and he tried his best to satisfy them.

My brother graduated from medical school a few

years ago which proves that he has lots of patience (and a few patients) as well as a capacity for hard work. Qualities he has needed in order to cope with these very different women. But he did so and successfully managed to transform romances into love affairs and then into stable relationships.

An interesting sidelight about my brother is his admiration for Spock, star of Star Trek. Robbie loves the objectivity, logic and sense of fair play demonstrated by his pointy-eared, Vulcan hero.

By nature, Robbie seems to have inherited these Vulcan qualities. Being incongruously lazy and self-indulgent as well, he has had to make a conscious effort to keep his good qualities in working order. I've observed that he is particularly diplomatic during arguments. He rarely loses his temper, always speaks calmly and makes a real effort to listen to the other person's point of view. Then he objectively tries to answer each argument with one of his own. He never baits the other person or throws out invectives that make the situation worse.

I'm not trying to paint the picture of a perfect angel because he is far from It. But these are positive qualities he has developed and learned to use with great advantage.

Here is an example of a fundamental compromise made by him. Robbie tends to get into a social rut and has been traditionally closed minded about trying different activities or broadening his small circle of friends.

Basically, he enjoys watching tv (especially Star Trek reruns) going to ball games, concerts or movies and eating in Chinese restaurants.

The women in his life have protested, mostly in vain. He was forced to give ground grudgingly in his first relationship. He has learned to be more experimental the second time around. He has even found out that dancing ain't that bad even if you are a bad dancer. He has also discovered that socializing with someone else's friends is a good way to make new friends, even if you're shy.

Basic? Yes, but sometimes it can be like pulling teeth to get certain people to vary their routines.

Trying something new may not always work. In fact, it may confirm your notion that it was a rotten idea in the first place. But you've still got to be loose enough to give it a try. Even if it's only for the other person's satisfaction. Sometimes, especially for that reason. You'd be surprised how often your partner just wants to be met half way — one time.

On the flip side, you may try something new and discover that you actually had a great time. Roller skating turned out to be fun even though it sounded crazy. Bingo wasn't such a dumb idea after all, you won. This is one of the benefits of becoming a twosome. It's a very broadening experience.

There are many other aspects to compromise and self-indulgence but first you must decide to deal with them and be willing to find a happy medium. In effect, that will be your first move toward compromising.

Make no mistake about it, without a fair balance, few relationships will last very long. And if you truly want to have a love to share your life, you must accept this. If you can't, odds are no one will be able to accept you.

Perseverance is the energy you'll need to continually work toward compromise and balance. It won't come easy on either side. Both of you will have to adjust your ideals because contrary to rumor, great relationships are not made in heaven (they may be inspired there) but they are made on earth. In the realities of imperfection, human frailty and differences of opinion. But you can learn from one another, modify your basic personality and grow as a human being without giving up your individuality.

As always, actions speak louder than words. Setting the right example will do more to convince your partner than long tedious arguments. Remembering special occasions go much farther than complaining about why the other person is so forgetful. Show someone how you want to be treated by treating them that way.

There are so many areas for compromise that it is crazy to attempt discussing them. You face them every day and new ones come along as you meet new people. But when you examine patterns in your own behavior, you may discover that a certain resistance turns up over and over again. Think about those moments of stubborness and imagine yourself giving in just a little. Sometimes a little is all it takes.

To Succeed In Love
You Must Succeed In Life

Henry Kissinger said, "Power is the greatest aphrodisiac." If someone as homely as Henry can become a notorious, international, lover-boy, there must be something to it.

There is no doubt that success is an attractive, sexy characteristic. It symbolizes security, ease and luxury, and it makes a very strong statement about the capabilities of the person who achieved it.

Succeeding in life is by no means limited to acquiring material possessions and bank accounts. To the greatest extent it means fulfilling your potential as a human being.

Since we each have a variety of special talents, our successes can be as individual as we are. There is admiration for the specialist whether he be an excellent brain surgeon or an excellent gardener. And there is another kind of admiration for the multifaceted individual who plunges into life in many directions and comes up a winner through sheer joie de vivre and energy.

Do you know anyone who attacks tennis and chess with the same enthusiasm as baking corn muffins, writing poetry or cleaning windows? Wouldn't you like to?

It is exciting to be with people who work hard and

play hard. Even when they aren't the greatest, we admire their passion for life. We want to be part of their world because we want it to rub off on us. We seek contact with these people so that we can learn and grow with them.

In the chapter "When you least expect it", I mentioned my good fortune in attracting two wonderful women during a work stint when I had allotted myself very little time for socializing. In retrospect, I realize that this and other highly productive periods in my life were generally the most socially productive as well.

There is no coincidence that when all systems are GO you feel a dynamic surge of energy that seeps into every aspect of your life. And people notice. Even if you aren't aware of it.

They see it, sense it and feel it. The way you walk, the confidence you project, the pride you radiate. I have great respect for any one who is both efficient and creative, whether it be in the office, the kitchen, the bedroom, the woods, the seashore or the athletic field.

I marvel at the courage and talent of musicians, actors and artists. People who put themselves on the line for any number of incredibly painful rejections and usually, very little money. They are all successes merely for trying. When they actually do succeed we call them stars.

There is no doubt that success in our careers makes us feel more potent and desirable. And we are. Partly, because we feel it, and in part, because our accomplishments represent something special to others.

Conversely, when we stagnate or suffer defeats continuously, a sense of impotence and ugliness saturates our souls.

I recently witnessed the dissolution of a seven year old marriage. We all could see it coming but it was still very sad when it finally happened.

Success for one and the lack of it for the other created a rift that eventually widened into a split. During their marriage, Joyce rose from photographer's secretary, to an assistant photographer, to a commercial designer and is now a photographer herself.

Her husband Jerry assisted a music promoter for several years putting on Oldies Rock 'n Roll shows. Then he became a partner in his own business selling CB radio equipment. By the time he had gotten his product ready to merchandise, the boom had passed him by. And his marriage went along with it. Jerry was always in there plugging but he never could quite get it together. He will though, he's only thirty.

Maybe society places undue stress on men to be successful but the reality is that it is expected of them. For a woman, dealing with success is a whole other matter. Most men aren't ready to cope with it, much less, most women.

My observations indicate that only strong, self-assured, successful men can handle successful women. Other men tend to be intimidated and put off one way or another.

As difficult as it was for Jerry to accept Joyce's success, her independence, busy schedule, even the money she earned, it was equally difficult for Joyce to deal with her husband's failures and frustration. Though she loved him, she slowly began to dominate him.

His frustration was manifested by running around with younger women who looked up to him. Eventually Joyce sought out older, more successful men who not only felt comfortable with her accomplishments but were attracted to her because of them.

Like water, we too, seek our own levels.

I believe hard work pays off in a multitude of ways. But I'm not saying there won't be problems.

I watched Freddy R., a funny little man with a floppy Buster Brown hairdo, glasses and bow ties go from laughable to enviable. He was a bit of a joke to his co-workers, partly because of his appearance, and partly because he worked so hard.

They laughed about his late hours in the office and his overtime weekends. But Freddy continued to move steadily up the executive ladder. By the time he was thirty-seven he was a vice president. People stopped laughing. All of a sudden he moved in on an exquisite woman who had recently been hired in the accounting department. To everyone's amazement, she not only went out with him, she married him six months later.

Could it be that Freddy was working so hard all those years to be worthy of the kind of wife he dreamed about attracting?

Most people admire diligent workers. Some may scoff because it makes them feel lazy and somewhat insecure by comparison. But deep down, they show respect.

On the cynical side you may say, we are attracted to successful people because they can help us or because we can use them. That's part of it but there's a lot more.

We are attracted to people who control their own destiny and make things happen instead of sitting back complaining and hoping.

Confidence breeds confidence. When we succeed on the battlefields of life, we suspect that we can succeed on the playing fields as well. And you know something, we can.

If you can accomplish most of the things you hope to in this life, you have an excellent chance of attracting the kind of lover you've always dreamed about. Then it will be your turn to change fantasy into reality.

Putting career accomplishments aside for a moment, let us also consider succeeding as a human being. Respecting the rights of others, attempting to deal fairly and honorably with people, treating them with kindness, tenderness, sensitivity and whenever possible, with love.

It is easier to follow these dictates if you believe in God as well as in yourself. God is love and this book would be incomplete without considering the pros and cons of leading a spiritual life.

There is much comfort, strength, solace and guidance in all religions. While the trappings and rituals may vary, the basic tenets remain very much the same. Without getting into a heavy religious discussion, let's just consider God in relation to the purpose of this book: How to find someone to love.

I'm not trying to convert anyone, I'm simply making another observation about love and how to find it. In my experience, people who believe in God and attempt to shape their lives accordingly have an easier time finding love, lovers and happiness.

In some ways you can compare the belief in God with the Philosophy of Hard Work. Even those who scoff, secretly admire the Workers and the Believers. Then, there are the millions who don't scoff at all but openly admire those who work hard, play hard and keep the faith.

It just takes guts, hard work, faith and a little bit of luck. That's all.

I just wish I could follow all this good advice myself. Sometimes it's a lot easier to be a philosopher than a practitioner. But it is possible to be both. And when you do, you'll connect.